ITU Library
Date: _____

Turbo® Pascal
DOS Utilities

RELATED TITLES OF INTEREST FROM JOHN WILEY & SONS

Jacobson	*Advanced Symphony: A Power User's Guide*
Skinner	*An Introduction to Assembly Language Programming for the 8086 Family*
Morse & Albert	*The 80286 Architecture*
Morse, Albert & Isaacson	*The 80386 Architecture*
Fernandez, Tabler & Ashley	*6502 Assembly Language Programming*
Miller & Quilici	*C Programming Language: An Applied Perspective*
Schwaderer	*C Wizard's Programming Reference*
Ashley & Fernandez	*COBOL Wizard: A Wiley Programmer's Reference*
Ashley & Fernandez	*COBOL for Microcomputers*
Ashley	*Structured COBOL*
Winfield	*The Complete Forth*
Greenberg & Greenberg	*The Complete Guide to dBase III*
Walden	*File Formats for Popular PC Software: A Programmer's Reference*
Stern	*Flowcharting: A Tool for Understanding Computer Logic*
Tabler	*IBM PC Assembly Language*
Brown & Finkel	*IBM PC Data File Programming*
Ashley & Fernandez	*JCL for IBM VSE Systems: A Self-Teaching Guide*
Williams	*Lotus 1-2-3 Release 2.0 ASAP*
Williams	*Lotus 1-2-3 from A to Z with Bridges to Symphony*
Wiener	*Modula-2 Wizard: A Wiley Programmer's Reference*
Crandall	*Pascal Applications for the Sciences*
Ashley & Fernandez	*PC DOS, 2nd Edition*
Sawyer & Foster	*Programming Expert Systems in Modula-2*
Sawyer & Foster	*Programming Expert Systems in Pascal*
Doyle	*Using Supercalc: The Next Generation*
Ashley & Fernandez	*WordStar and WordStar 2000: Advanced Tips & Techniques*
Ashley & Fernandez & Sansom	*WordStar Without Tears*

Turbo® Pascal DOS Utilities

Robert Alonso

John Wiley & Sons, Inc.
New York • Chichester • Brisbane • Toronto • Singapore

Publisher: Stephen Kippur
Editor: Therese A. Zak
Managing Editor: Andrew B. Hoffer
Electronic Production Services: The Publisher's Network

This publication is designed to provide accurate and authoritative information in regard to the subject matter covered. It is sold with the understanding that the publisher is not engaged in rendering professional advice. If professional advice or other expert assistance is required, the services of a competent professional person should be sought.

Turbo is a registered trademark of Borland, Inc.

Copyright © 1987 by John Wiley & Sons, Inc.

All rights reserved. Published simultaneously in Canada.

Reproduction or translation of any part of this work beyond that permitted by Section 107 or 108 of the 1976 United States Copyright Act without the permission of the copyright owner is unlawful. Requests for permission or further information should be addressed to the Permissions Department, John Wiley & Sons, Inc.

Library of Congress Cataloging in Publication Data

Alonso, Robert.
   Turbo Pascal DOS utilities.

   Includes index.
   1. PASCAL (Computer program language) 2. Turbo Pascal (Computer program) 3. Utilities (Computer programs) 4. MS-DOS (Computer operating system) 5. PC DOS (Computer operating system) I. Title
   QA76.73.P2A5   1987   005.4'46   87-2135
   ISBN 0-471-85995-8

Printed in the United States of America
87 88 10 9 8 7 6 5 4 3 2 1

Dedicated to my wife, Elva.

Contents

Chapter 1	Introduction	1
Chapter 2	**General Utilities**	4
	BEEP 4	
	CAL 9	
	COLOR 13	
	FUNKEYS 19	
	HELP 24	
	KEYS 36	
	LPRINT 41	
Chapter 3	**File Utilities**	44
	COUNT 44	
	CREATE 50	
	DETAB 55	
	ENCODE 60	
	LLIST 67	
	WSASCII 72	
Chapter 4	**System Utilities**	77
	ALTER 77	
	DIAG 84	
	DISECT 94	
	FINDFILE 103	
	MOVE 112	
Chapter 5	**Peripheral Utilities**	116
	LASER 116	
	PMODE 122	

Chapter 6	Procedures and Functions—Programming Notes	128
	BEEPTONE 128	
	CALLCHMOD 129	
	CHECKMEMORYSIZE 130	
	CLOSEFILES 131	
	CONVERTTOSCALAR 131	
	COPYRIGHT 132	
	DOIO 134	
	DOSVERSION 134	
	EMSCHECK 135	
	ENCODECHARACTERS 136	
	ERROR 137	
	EXIST 138	
	FINDFIRST 138	
	FINDNEXT 139	
	HELP 139	
	HEX 140	
	INITIALIZE 140	
	MACHINETYPE 141	
	MOVEIT 141	
	OPENFILES 142	
	PARSECOMMANDLINE 142	
	PRINTLN 142	
	ROMDATE 143	
	SECTORWRITE 143	
	SETDTA 144	
	UPITSCASE 145	
	YES 145	
Appendix A	**How to Compile**	**147**
Appendix B	**Installing the Compiled Utilities**	**157**
	Making a Backup to a Hard Disk 157	
	Setting Up a Path Command 158	
Index		**159**

CHAPTER 1

Introduction

Until the recent success of Turbo Pascal, Pascal was a computer language reserved for university curriculums. It was and continues to be regarded as the language of choice for education. The reason Pascal has been so successful in the schools is that it is a very structured language that forces the programmer to think about what steps the program must take to arrive at the desired result and what type of data will be needed. All versions of Pascal, including Turbo, require that the programmer declare procedures and functions and all the types, constants, and variables that the program will use. Many believe that all the planning that Pascal requires stifles the creativity of novices and makes many choose not to continue their study of programming. Unfortunately, in some cases the belief may be true, but for those who can work with the structured environment that Pascal creates, there are many rewards. Pascal, and particularly Turbo Pascal, can be used to create hundreds of useful programs quickly and efficiently. Its flexibility can make it the ideal language for utilities like the ones presented in this book or even for complete application programs.

Pascal derives its name from the seventeenth-century mathematician Blaise Pascal, but its inventor is Niklaus Wirth. Wirth, a professor from the Technical University in Zurich, Switzerland defined the Pascal language in 1971. Turbo Pascal is an implementation of that definition with some additions for direct access to the memory and port address space of the computer, low-level access to the operating system, graphics, and color. These additions have made Turbo Pascal one of the most versatile languages for the IBM PC. In addition to giving you control of the entire machine with its low-level operating system access, Turbo makes it easier to write programs for the IBM PC because it requires no link process: Source code is converted into executable command files in one incredibly fast process. Turbo Pascal's compilation speed and error checking have made the Pascal language easier to learn and understand as well as a more desirable alternative to interpreted languages such as BASIC.

The more powerful utilities in this book take advantage of many of the enhancements that Turbo Pascal has given the Pascal language. These utilities are examples of the power that Turbo has given the ordinary high-level-language programmer. Without having to write assembler routines that are linkable and that must follow strict guidelines, the Turbo programmer can have the same control of the machine through the **MsDOS** command. The real breadth of Turbo Pascal and its overwhelming superiority to BASIC is manifested in utilities such as **Diag** and **Findfile.** These two utilities would be impossible to write in BASIC. Neither the compiled nor interpreted versions of BASIC give the programmer the necessary control of the operating system to make such a utility possible.

Turbo Pascal is such an efficient programming environment that it can even run on such limited machines as the IBM PCjr (a miraculous achievement for a compiler). It generates MS-DOS command files (files ending with **.COM**) that can be made to look and work like the DOS commands that Microsoft provides. Each utility in this book is thus designed to mimic DOS (Disk Operating System) commands as much as possible. Like DOS commands, each utility requires all input to be from the command line. That means that you type all the necessary information after the utility's name and separate the information with spaces—exactly as you would do with DOS commands. Since all but one of the utilities in this book are designed to work this way, you can include them in batch files to really streamline your work. There won't be any pauses in the middle of your batch process to ask you to input a file name or any other type of information. The only way that these utilities differ from standard DOS commands is that they include built-in help text. If you forget how to use a utility or what format the command line expects, you simply type its name at the command prompt, and it will print out a clear explanation of what it does and how it expects input from you. Each explanation will also give you an example of how to use it. This is one feature that many wish Microsoft would include in all its DOS commands.

Perhaps the best feature of these utilities is that you can modify them to work exactly to your liking. The source code is full of explanations and comments to make it easy for you to modify. Some of the utilities are designed to work with specific hardware configurations, like an IBM graphics printer or a Hewlett Packard LaserJet printer. Since the source code is provided, you can easily modify these hardware specific utilities to work with whatever hardware you use. Whenever a utility works only with a name brand product, it does so because that product has proven itself to be superior in quality and extremely popular.

The disks that can be ordered with this book include both the source code and compiled code for every utility in this book. This means that if you have the Turbo Pascal compiler you can tinker with the utilities and recompile them. If you don't, though, you can still make use of the utilities by ordering the disks through the mail. The reason that the disks have been made available is that you may not want to bother with programming at all; you may just want one or more of the included utilities. If this is the case, then it is only fair to provide a sensible alternative to purchasing both this book and a compiler that you may use only once. Whichever is the case, having both available is probably a good way to ensure that you will get your money's worth. Just remember that to use them you must use DOS version 2.0 or greater. The utilities have been tested on DOS versions ranging from 2.0 to 3.21 and work in IBM equipment as well as compatibles with at least 64K of memory. The Turbo Pascal version that the utilities were written under was 3.01A.

Once you have the compiled utilities ready, you may want to place them either on your start-up diskette or in a subdirectory of your hard disk. For floppy disk drive users, it is a good idea to keep the utilities on a disk that contains **COMMAND.COM**, the command interpreter that MS and PC-DOS machines require to function properly. For the most part, these utilities use the high portion of memory and will overwrite what is called the transient portion of the command processor. When you finish using a Turbo utility, DOS will require that **COMMAND.COM** be present so that it can load it from disk to replace what Turbo Pascal has corrupted. This corruption is caused by the way the compiler forces the utilities to use memory and can't be controlled by the programmer. Therefore it is advisable to have the command interpreter on each disk that contains Turbo Pascal utilities. Another alternative, for hard disk users, is to copy these utilities to the root directory of the disk or to a subdirectory that contains DOS or some other utilities or even the directory where the Turbo Pascal compiler is stored. In either case, if the command interpreter is present on the disk, you will not notice anything. The operating system automatically fetches a new copy of the transient portion of the interpreter. If when you execute one of the utilities you get an error message that tells you that an "I/O error" has occurred, look it up in Appendix G of the Turbo Pascal Reference Manual. It usually is nothing to get concerned about and will almost never happen under normal conditions.

If you are interested only in the utilities, then you are practically done. You can read Appendix B, "Installing the Compiled Utilities," to get some further instructions on how to use the utilities in an effective way on a hard disk. Otherwise, read on for details on how to use the utilities, the programming techniques used to produce them, and the commented source code listings.

CHAPTER 2

General Utilities

BEEP

Type External

Purpose This command produces a tone. It can be used to draw attention to the screen in batch files.

Format BEEP
or
BEEB num1

The term *num1* can be in the range 0 to 32767.

One of the features lacking in Microsoft DOS is the ability to draw attention to the screen with a command that produces a sound. A sound can be quite useful when several commands are included in a batch file and some may cause unrecoverable damage to either data or programs. For example, if you create a batch file for deleting backups that your word processor automatically produces (see Example 1), you will need a way to prompt the user of that batch file—whether it is yourself or not—that some files are about to be deleted from the disk and that special attention should be placed on the screen. BEEP is designed specifically to draw as much attention as necessary: You can make it produce an irritating tone as many as 32,767 times in a row. But depending on the circumstances, you will probably need to produce between 1 and 3 tones only.

BEEP by itself on the command line will print a help screen for the command.

Example 1—Batch file for deleting backup files (.bak)

```
echo off
echo This batch file will purge your
echo disk of unwanted .BAK files.
echo Insert the disk in drive B:.
beep 1
pause
```

```
echo The following is in the directory of
echo the disk in drive B:.
dir b:/w
beep 5
echo Do you wish to delete the .BAK
echo files on the disk? Press any key
echo to continue or CONTROL C to end.
beep 1
pause
del b:*.bak
echo Files have been deleted.
echo on
```

Example 2—Batch file for formatting diskettes

```
echo off
echo This batch file will format
echo diskettes on drive B:.
beep 1
echo Insert a blank diskette in B:.
beep 1
pause
echo Are you sure it is a blank disk?
echo If you do not wish to continue then
echo press CONTROL C.
beep 5
pause
format b:
echo Disk in B: now formatted.
echo on
```

Program

```
Program Beep;
{
    Title       : BEEP SOUND MAKER    Version 2.00
    Author      : Robert Alonso
    Versions    : 1.00 September 28, 1985
                  2.00 October 7, 1985

    Purpose     : This program produces a beep sound. The
                  command line is parsed for the number of
                  beep tones to produce.
```

(continued)

I/O Requirements : The program will work on MS-DOS and PC-DOS computers that accept ASCII character 7 as a bell sound.
}

```pascal
const
  bell     = #7;          { ASCII character for bell sound. }
  time     = 100;         { Delay time between tones.       }


var
  i            : integer;      { Integer used in loop structure. }
  Number       : integer;      { Number of times to produce tone. }
  Result       : integer;      { Result of converting string parameter
                                 to an integer format with Val. }
  CommandLine  : string[128];  { Maximum length of DOS parameter. }
```

{
"Error" is a procedure that outputs text when the program's
input is unacceptable. This procedure will be invoked when the
command line parameter is a value less than 1 or greater than
32767. It will also be invoked if any strange characters interfere
with the string to integer conversion function Val. All output is
sent to the current output device--usually the screen.
}

```pascal
procedure Error;
begin
  writeln;
  writeln('An error has occurred. Please use only numbers');
  writeln('after the command "beep." Any number greater');
  writeln('than 0, but less than 32768 is valid. Letters');
  writeln('will cause an error.');
end;
```

{
"Help" is a procedure that outputs text that guides the program's
user. All output is sent to the current output device--usually the
screen.
}

```
procedure Help;
begin
  writeln;
  writeln('BEEP draws attention to the screen by producing');
  writeln('a tone. It can be included in batch files and');
  writeln('called just before a dangerous command is');
  writeln('executed (ie.,FORMAT). BEEP will sound as many');
  writeln('times as you specify. Example: A>BEEP number');
  writeln;
  writeln('Only numbers should be typed after "beep."');
end;
```

```
{
  "BeepTone" is the procedure that prints an ASCII character 7 to
  produce the beep tone. A delay is also used to allow time between
  each tone.
}
```

```
procedure BeepTone;
begin
  write (bell);
  delay (time);
end;
```

```
{
  "ParseLine" is a procedure that parses the DOS command line and
  extracts an integer value that represents the number of time that
  the beep tone is repeated. A lack of a parameter executes the "Help"
  procedure and halts program execution. Any invalid parameter causes
  execution of the "Error" procedure.
}
```

(continued)

```pascal
procedure ParseLine;
begin
  if ParamCount = 0
    then
      begin
        Help;
        Halt;
      end
    else
      begin
        Number := 0;
        CommandLine := ParamStr(1);
        val (CommandLine, Number, Result);
        if (Result <> 0) or (Number < 1)
          then Error;
      end;
end;

{
    "ProduceSound" is a procedure that produces the sound by calling
    the "BeepTone" procedure.
}


procedure ProduceSound;
begin
  for i := 1 to Number do
    BeepTone;
end;


begin   {Main Program}
  ParseLine;
  ProduceSound;
end.
```

CAL

Type	External
Purpose	This utility allows you to make quick calculations from the DOS command line. Addition, subtraction, multiplication, and division are allowed.
Format	CAL *or* CAL num1 + num2 *or* CAL num1 − num2 *or* CAL num1 * num2 *or* CAL num1 / num2

The terms *num1* and *num2* are real numbers. This means that you can use numbers with decimal points. For example, you could calculate the difference between 2.55 and 1.13.

Certain rules have to be followed when using this command. Always insert a space after the command name and between each number and the operation symbol. For example, if you wanted to calculate 100 times 2547.33, you would type **CAL** at the command prompt followed by a space, then **100** followed by another space, the asterisk (signifies multiplication), another space, and finally **2547.33**.
It would look as follows:

A>cal 100 * 2547.33

CAL is for those moments when you do not have a calculator handy. Although DOS is extremely powerful, it lacks a way to do simple calculations from the command line, which is probably one of the reasons that Borland has done so well with its pop-up program Sidekick. You can use CAL like any other external DOS command. It will let you add, subtract, multiply, and divide numbers. And it does not have any difficulty with very large numbers, or with small numbers, and it accepts numbers with decimal places.

Example 1—Getting help on the command

    A>cal
    help text is printed

Example 2—Adding two numbers

    A>cal 32 + 25.7
    Answer = 57.70

Example 3—Dividing numbers

    A>cal 100 / 3
    Answer = 33.33

Program

```
Program Cal;
{
    Title         : CALCULATE COMMAND LINE    Version 2.00
    Author        : Robert Alonso
    Versions      : 1.00 October 5, 1985
                    2.00 October 8, 1985

    Purpose       : This program allows simple calculations from
                    the command line. The DOS command line is
                    parsed for two numbers and an operator.

    I/O Requirements : The program will work on MS-DOS and PC-DOS
                    computers. It expects two numbers and an
                    operator as input from the command line and
                    gives the answer as output directed to the
                    screen.
}

var
   Number1    :real;   { These are extracted from the command line arguments }
   Number2    :real;   { in string format and then are converted to reals.   }
   Answer     :real;
   Operator   :char;   { The operator can only be one character in size.     }
   Outstring  :string[255];
   Result1    :integer; { The are used to keep track of whether an error     }
   Result2    :integer; { occurred during the processing of the numbers.     }

{
   "Error" is a procedure that outputs text that guides the program's
   user when an error occurs. All output is sent to the current output
   device--usually the screen.
}
```

```
procedure Error;
begin
  writeln;
  writeln('The format of the expression to be calculated');
  writeln('is incorrect. You must first enter "CAL"');
  writeln('followed by a space, then the first number,');
  writeln('another space, the operator , another space,');
  writeln('and finally the second number.');
  writeln;
  writeln('Valid example: A>CAL 10 + 5');
  writeln('The only valid operators are: +,-,/,*.');
  Halt;
end;
```

{
  "Help" is a procedure that outputs text that guides the program's
  user. All output is sent to the current output device--usually the
  screen.
}

```
procedure Help;
begin
  writeln;
  writeln('CAL allows you to do quick additions,');
  writeln('subtractions, multiplications and divisions');
  writeln('from the command line. Example: CAL 2 / 4');
  Halt;
end;
```

{
  "ParseLine" is a procedure that extracts all the necessary input
  from the command line. Two numbers and an operator are extracted
  or the "Help" procedure is called. "Error" is called if the operator
  is more than one character in length or if an error occurs during
  the conversion of the command line strings into real numbers.
}

```
procedure ParseLine;
begin
  if ParamCount = 0
    then Help
    else
      begin
        Number1 := 0;
        Number2 := 0;
        if length (ParamStr(2)) = 1
          then
            begin
              Operator := ParamStr(2);
```

(continued)

```pascal
            val (ParamSTR(1), Number1, Result1);
            val (ParamSTR(3), Number2, Result2);
            if (Result1 <> 0) or (Result2 <> 0)
              then Error;
          end
        else Error;
    end;
end;


{
  "ProcessData" is a procedure that performs the required operation on
  the input.
}


procedure ProcessData;
begin
  case Operator of
    '+': Answer := Number1 + Number2;
    '-': Answer := Number1 - Number2;
    '/': Answer := Number1 / Number2;
    '*': Answer := Number1 * Number2;
  else Error;
  end;
end;


{
  "ReportResult" is a procedure that first formats the result from the
  "ProcessData" procedure and then outputs the answer to the screen.
}


procedure ReportResult;
begin
  str (Answer:0:2, Outstring); { Make it have only two decimal places. }
  writeln;
  writeln('Answer = ',Outstring);
end;


begin    {Main Program}
  ParseLine;
  ProcessData;
  ReportResult;
end.
```

COLOR

Type External

Purpose This program changes the background, foreground, and border colors of the screen of an IBM-compatible machine.

Format COLOR
or
COLOR foreground background border

Any of the three parameters can be one of the following colors:

Black	Blue	Green
Cyan	Red	Magenta
Brown	LightGray	DarkGray
LightBlue	LightGreen	LightCyan
LightRed	LightMagenta	Yellow
White		

Case does not matter because a routine in the program will automatically convert all input parameters to uppercase.

It is not often that one runs across a utility for setting the color of the IBM display. The reason for this is probably that since two thirds of all PCs are used with a monochrome monitor, very few programmers have seen a need for one. None of these monochrome monitors can use a program that changes colors, but for the third that does have a color monitor, a program like this can be both fun and useful. Its main utility is in giving you a choice over the colors you use in DOS. This can reduce eyestrain—and also give you one more excuse for having purchased a color monitor.

Using the program is very easy. You just type the word **COLOR** at the command prompt and specify your three color choices. Each of these choices must be separated by a space so that the program can parse them into three distinct choices. If you ever need help with the utility, you can just type **COLOR** alone, and a help message will be printed.

Example 1—Getting help

   A>color
   help text is printed

Example 2—Setting the foreground color to green, background to red, and border to brown

A>color green red brown

Example 3—Setting the foreground color to cyan, background to magenta, and border to lightgray

A>color cyan magenta lightgray

Program

```
Program Colors;

{
    Title       : CHANGE COLORS      Version 2.00
    Author      : Robert Alonso
    Versions    : 1.00 February 20, 1986

    Purpose     : This program changes the background, foreground
                  and border colors of the screen of an IBM
                  compatible machine.

    I/O Requirements : Three parameters must be given to this program
                       for it to work properly. All three; the background,
                       foreground, and border color choices are fed
                       into the program at the MS or PC-DOS command line.

    Allowed parameters are :

    Black       Blue            Green
    Cyan        Red             Magenta
    Brown       LightGray       DarkGray
    LightBlue   LightGreen      LightCyan
    LightRed    LightMagenta    Yellow
    White
}
type
  ColorType = (Black,Blue,Green,
               Cyan,Red,Magenta,
               Brown,LightGray,DarkGray,
               LightBlue,LightGreen,LightCyan,
               LightRed,LightMagenta,Yellow,
               White,NotValid);
  InString  = string[12];
  MaxString = string[255];

var
  Code      : ColorType;
  ColorIn   : array [ColorType] of InString;
  Mode,
  InFore,
```

```pascal
    InBack,
    InBorder  : InString;
    Fore,
    Back,
    Border,
    Choice    : byte;
    Found     : boolean;
    Regs      :
      record
        AL, AH, BL, BH, CL, CH, DL, DH : byte;
      end;
```

{
"Help" is a procedure that outputs text that guides the program's
user. All output is sent to the current output device--usually the
screen.
}

```pascal
procedure Help;
begin
  writeln;
  writeln('COLOR allows you to set the foreground,');
  writeln('background and border colors of you monitor.');
  writeln('To use it, just type COLOR followed by three');
  writeln('of the allowed parameters. ');
  writeln('Example: A>color red green brown');
  writeln;
  writeln('The following are valid parameters:');
  writeln;
  writeln('Black          Blue           Green          Cyan');
  writeln('Red            Magenta        Brown          LightGray');
  writeln('DarkGray       LightBlue      LightGreen     LightCyan');
  writeln('LightRed       LightMagenta   Yellow         White');
  Halt;
end;
```

{
"Error" is a procedure that outputs text when the program's
input is unacceptable. This procedure will be invoked when there
are to few parameters on the command line or when the parameters
have no corresponding match in the array of valid parameters.
}

```pascal
procedure Error;
begin
  writeln;
  writeln('An error has occurred. Please make sure that');
  writeln('three color choices follow the word COLOR on the');
  writeln('command line. Example: A>color red green brown');
  writeln;
  writeln('Also make sure that you are using valid color');
  writeln('choices. For help and a complete list of valid');
  writeln('colors, type "COLOR" by itself at the command line');
```

(continued)

```
        Halt;
end;


{
  "UpItsCase" is a function that takes a string of any length and
  sets all of the characters in the string to upper case. Its handy
  for comparing strings.
}

function UpItsCase (SourceStr : MaxString) : MaxString;
var
   I        : integer;
begin
  for I := 1 to length(SourceStr) do
     SourceStr[I] := UpCase(SourceStr[I]);
  UpItsCase := SourceStr
end;


{
  "ConvertToScalar" is a function that is used for converting input
  strings to a defined scalar type, "ColorType."
}

function ConvertToScalar(Mode : InString) : byte;
begin
  Found  := False;
  Code   := Black;
  Choice := 0;
  repeat
    if ColorIn[Code] = Mode
      then Found := True
      else
        begin
          Code := Succ(Code);
          Choice := Choice + 1;
        end;
  until Found or (Code = NotValid);
  if not Found
    then Error
    else ConvertToScalar := Choice;
end;


{
  "ParseCommandLine" is a procedure that checks if any data was input
  at the DOS command line. If no data is there, then the "Help"
  procedure is executed and the program is halted. Otherwise, three
  variables are set equal to the three parameters in the command line.
  If there are less than three parameters, the "Error' procedure is
  executed.
}
```

```
procedure ParseCommandLine;
begin
 if ParamCount = 0
   then Help
   else
      if ParamCount <> 3
        then Error
        else
          begin
            InFore   := ParamStr(1);
            InBack   := ParamStr(2);
            InBorder := ParamStr(3);
            Infore   := UpItsCase(Infore);   { Need to get the uppercase    }
            InBack   := UpItsCase(InBack);   { version of the input strings }
            InBorder := UpItsCase(InBorder); { for later comparisons.       }
          end;
end;
```

{
  "Initialize" does exactly what the name implies. It is used in this
  utility to intialize an array that is used in converting strings to
  the defined scalar type, "ColorType."
}

```
procedure Initialize;
begin
  ColorIn[Black]        := 'BLACK';
  ColorIn[Blue]         := 'BLUE';
  ColorIn[Green]        := 'GREEN';
  ColorIn[Cyan]         := 'CYAN';
  ColorIn[Red]          := 'RED';
  ColorIn[Magenta]      := 'MAGENTA';
  ColorIn[Brown]        := 'BROWN';
  ColorIn[LightGray]    := 'LIGHTGRAY';
  ColorIn[DarkGray]     := 'DARKGRAY';
  ColorIn[LightBlue]    := 'LIGHTBLUE';
  ColorIn[LightGreen]   := 'LIGHTGREEN';
  ColorIn[LightCyan]    := 'LIGHTCYAN';
  ColorIn[LightRed]     := 'LIGHTRED';
  ColorIn[LightMagenta] := 'LIGHTMAGENTA';
  ColorIn[Yellow]       := 'YELLOW';
  ColorIn[White]        := 'WHITE';
  ColorIn[NotValid]     := 'NOTVALID';
end;
```

{
  "Convert_All_Input_To_Scalars" is used for calling the similarly
  named function to convert the various input strings. The routine's
  purpose is to keep the main program loop tidy.
}

(continued)

```pascal
procedure Convert_All_Input_To_Scalars;
begin
  Fore   := ConvertToScalar(InFore);
  Back   := ConvertToScalar(InBack);
  Border := ConvertToScalar(InBorder);
end;

{
  "ChangeColors" uses a BIOS call to set the border color and then uses
  two built in Turbo Pascal V 3.0 procedures to set the foreground and
  background color.
}

procedure ChangeColors;
begin
  Regs.AH := 11;
  Regs.BH := 0;
  Regs.BL := Border;
  Intr($10,Regs);

  textcolor(Fore);
  textbackground(Back);
  ClrScr;              { Needed or color won't take control of screen. }
end;


begin   {Main}
  Initialize;
  ParseCommandLine;
  Convert_All_Input_To_Scalars;
  ChangeColors;
end.
```

FUNKEYS

Type External

Purpose This utility lets you set the function keys or, with some work, any other key to whatever set of characters you would like. With this program you will be able to customize the function keys to perform meaningful tasks.

Format FUNKEYS

This utility, unlike the others in the book, helps you extract a feature that is already available to you in DOS. Although few know about its existence, ANSI.SYS is a driver program that you can attach to DOS and use to perform many useful tasks. One of these tasks is the redefiniton of the keyboard. FUNKEYS makes use of this feature and also simplifies redefining keys by sheltering you from the nitty-gritty of how it is actually done. You could, for example, give FUNKEYS to someone who has never heard about ANSI.SYS and who really does not want to know and that person could still make good use of the program.

For you to fully understand what FUNKEYS does and how it does it, some preliminary explanation about DOS is necessary. When you insert a PC-DOS disk into your computer and turn the computer on, several things happen. First, the computer performs a power-on self-test (POST). This test checks the amount of memory and some other things important to the operation of the computer. Once the test is finished, the bootstrap loader is invoked. This routine loads a sector of code from the disk in drive A or C (depending on whether you have a hard disk). The sector that is loaded is called the boot record. Its function is to load a hidden DOS file called IBMBIO.COM. This file supplements some of the routines built into a ROM chip called the BIOS. It remains resident while you use the computer and performs several different functions. At boot time, it is in charge of scanning the disk for a file called CONFIG.SYS and executing the configuration instructions that the file contains. One instruction that the file can have is DEVICE = ANSI.SYS. The file must contain this instruction for FUNKEYS to work later. If IBMBIO.COM finds CONFIG.SYS and it contains instructions in it, it loads the device files (such as ANSI.SYS) and attaches them to itself. Next it loads another hidden DOS file called IBMDOS.COM and then COMMAND.COM, which is the command processor that we are familiar with. As you can see, getting DOS loaded is a long and complex process. Fortunately, it is also a fairly quick and invisible process. Machines running various different MS-DOS implementations all go through the same procedure but sometimes use hidden files with different names such as MSDOS.SYS for IBMDOS.COM. This should not matter to you, the user, though.

FUNKEYS needs ANSI.SYS. If you neglect to place the words DEVICE = ANSI.SYS in your CONFIG.SYS file, FUNKEYS will do nothing. ANSI.SYS is a general-purpose interface to some of the features of a machine's BIOS ROM chip, and it accepts escape codes as commands to modify the screen colors or keys on the keyboard. Because it accepts escape codes, it makes it very easy to make useful modifications to your system without resorting to assembly language programs or an intimate knowledge of how to execute BIOS calls. FUNKEYS sends escape calls to ANSI.SYS by sending its output to the screen through a DOS interrupt 21. The normal WRITELN procedure is not used because Turbo Pascal apparently bypasses DOS and uses the BIOS ROM chip through interrupt 10 to print things on the screen. Since ANSI.SYS is a part of DOS, DOS must not be bypassed.

Example 1—How to create a CONFIG.SYS file on your boot disk if one does not already exist: Press function key 6 or press the CTRL key and letter Z simultaneously to end the file.

```
A>copy con:config.sys
DEVICE = ANSI.SYS
^Z
```

Example 2—How to create a CONFIG.SYS file on your boot disk if one does not already exist: Another way is to use the utility in this book called CREATE.

```
A>create config.sys
```
Pressing Control "Z" saves the file to disk:
```
---- + ---- + ---- + ---- + ---- + ---- + ---- + ---- + ---- + ---- + ---- + ---- + ---- + ----
DEVICE = ANSI.SYS
^Z
```

Example 3—If CONFIG.SYS already exists, you must change it, not overwrite it. Use the Turbo Pascal editor to edit the file.

```
A>turbo
```
error message file not needed

Press E for edit and give Turbo the drive and name of the file. For example, if you loaded Turbo from your A: drive and have your boot disk temporarily in B:, type B:CONFIG.SYS to load and edit the CONFIG.SYS file. Add the line DEVICE = CONFIG.SYS and press CTRL KD followed by S to save the changed file.

Example 4—Getting help on the command

```
A>funkeys
```
message is printed

Example 5—Executing the command

A>funkeys
command is executed and message is printed (same as above)

If you see strange codes on your screen, then ANSI.SYS was not installed properly on your computer. The strange codes will be printed to the screen but will not be visible if all is right.

Program

```
Program Funkeys;
{
    Title        : FUNCTION KEY REDEFINER Version 1.00
    Author       : Robert Alonso
    Versions     : 1.00 February 9, 1986

    Purpose      : This program redefines the function keys
                   for use in the DOS environment.

    I/O Requirements : The program will work on MS-DOS and PC-DOS
                       computers that have the following in their
                       config.sys file:

                           DEVICE = ANSI.SYS

                       This makes the ansi screen driver become
                       attached to the system and facilitates the
                       redefinition of keys.
}
type
  string255 = string[255];
  RegRec    =
    record case integer of
      1: (AX, BX, CX, DX, BP, DI, SE, DS, ES, Flags : Integer);
      2: (AL, AH, BL, BH, CL, CH, DL, DH : Byte);
    end;

var
  Regs       : RegRec;
  Initstring : string[4];
  key1, key2, key3,
  key4, key5, key6,
  key7, key8, key9,
  key10      : string[25];
  Escape,
  Endstring  : string[2];


{
  This "Help" routine is not strictly used as a way to deliver
  information that will help the user with this program, but rather
```

(continued)

as a way to let the user know that the program has worked and
that everything is working fine. Since this program is so obvious
to use, no error handling routine is included either.
}

procedure Help;
begin
  writeln;
  writeln('FUNKEYS has just done it"s job! Your function');
  writeln('keys should now be redefined completely. Test');
  writeln('function key number 1 to make sure that all is');
  writeln('working properly. You should get the directory');
  writeln('of the current drive.');
  writeln;
  writeln('If the function keys are not redefined, then');
  writeln('read the book to follow the instructions on');
  writeln('how to install ANSI.SYS in your CONFIG.SYS file.');
end;

{
  "Println" is an alternative to the built in procedure, "writeln."
  The reason for incorporating it into this program is that Turbo
  Pascal apparently does not use DOS function 9 of interrupt 21
  for its routine. Using function 9 is necessary for sending escape
  sequences to the ANSI.SYS driver.
}

procedure Println(Instring : string255);
begin
  Regs.DX := Ofs(Instring)+1;
  Regs.DS := Seg(Instring);
  Regs.AH := 9;
  MsDos(Regs);
end;

{
  "Initialize" serves an obvious purpose. All variables are set
  equal to values that either the program requires or to desired
  values as in the key1 through key10. You can change the text
  within the single quotes in the assignments to key1 through key10
  so that those keys will print what you want on the screen.
}

```
procedure Initialize;
begin
  Escape := #27;
  Initstring := Escape + '[0;';
  Endstring := 'p$';              { The dollar symbol is needed as an }
  key1  := "DIR /P"';             { end delimeter for strings to be   }
  key2  := "CLS"';                { displayed with DOS function 9.    }
  key3  := "'COPY *.* "';
  key4  := "'DISKCOPY A: B:"';
  key5  := "'CD"';
  key6  := "'TYPE "';
  key7  := "'A:"';
  key8  := "'B:"';
  key9  := "'C:"';
  key10 := "'RENAME oldname newname"';
end;


{
  This routine calls the "Println" routine to output the string
  represented by the additions of characters within the brackets.
}


procedure PrintEscapeSequences;
begin
  println (Initstring+'59;'+key1+Endstring);
  println (Initstring+'60;'+key2+Endstring);
  println (Initstring+'61;'+key3+Endstring);
  println (Initstring+'62;'+key4+Endstring);
  println (Initstring+'63;'+key5+Endstring);
  println (Initstring+'64;'+key6+Endstring);
  println (Initstring+'65;'+key7+Endstring);
  println (Initstring+'66;'+key8+Endstring);
  println (Initstring+'67;'+key9+Endstring);
  println (Initstring+'68;'+key10+Endstring);
end;


begin {main}
  Initialize;
  PrintEscapeSequences;
  Help;
end.
```

HELP

Type	External
Purpose	This utility provides help to users of MS-DOS and PC-DOS computers. All the significant commands are included.
Format	HELP *or* HELP command

The *command* can be one of the following:

backup	del	graphics	rmdir
chdir	dir	mkdir	rd
cd	diskcomp	md	rename
chkdsk	diskcopy	mode	restore
cls	edlin	more	sort
comp	erase	path	time
copy	find	print	type
date	format	prompt	ver');

Unlike other complex programs that have pop-up help screens and context-sensitive guidance, DOS has no help facility for any of its commands. And what makes this odder yet is that it is very easy to argue that DOS is the most complex program that you run on a PC. Using a menu-driven program such as Lotus 1-2-3 is child's play by comparison. A user has almost no recourse but to plow through page after page of definitions and parameters and exceptions just to find out if a command can be useful for a particular application. This HELP utility tries to remedy the problem to a degree. It will give you a quick explanation of what a command can do and some information on the most useful parameters that you should know.

HELP is not all emcompassing; instead it provides you with quick information on the most necessary DOS commands. Since each help message is separated into its own procedure block, you can go in and modify the message to anything you like or expand on the messages. You could easily create entire help screens for each command.

HELP will not only provide help on the DOS commands, it will also give you help on how to use it. Just type HELP at the command line, and you will get it.

Example 1—Getting help on the command

    A>help
    help text is printed

Example 2—Getting help for the DOS command DIR
A> help dir
help text for DIR is printed

Example 3—Getting help for the DOS command COPY
A> help copy
help text for COPY is printed

Program

```
Program Help;
{
    Title      : HELP TEXT PRINTER     Version 1.00
    Author     : Robert Alonso
    Versions   : 1.00 May 13, 1986

    Purpose    : This program prints out help text for some
                 of the most common DOS commands.

    I/O Requirements : The program will work on IBM compatible
                       computers that run MS-DOS or PC-DOS.
}
type
  ModeType = (backupproc,chdirproc,cdproc,chkdskproc,clsproc,compproc,
              copyproc,dateproc,delproc,dirproc,diskcompproc,diskcopyproc,
              edlinproc,eraseproc,findproc,formatproc,graphicsproc,
              mkdirproc,mdproc,modeproc,moreproc,pathproc,printproc,
              promptproc,rmdirproc,rdproc,renameproc,restoreproc,sortproc,
              timeproc,typeproc,verproc,NotValid);

  MaxString = string[255];

var
  Code     : ModeType;
  HelpCode : string[8];
  ModeIn   : array [ModeType] of string[12];
  Found    : boolean;


{
  "UpItsCase" is a function that takes a string of any length and
  sets all of the characters in the string to upper case. Its handy
  for comparing strings.
}

function UpItsCase (SourceStr : MaxString) : MaxString;
var
  I      : integer;
```

(continued)

```
begin
  for I := 1 to length(SourceStr) do
    SourceStr[I] := UpCase(SourceStr[I]);
  UpItsCase := SourceStr
end;
```

{
  "Error" is a procedure that outputs text when the program's
  input is unacceptable. This procedure will be invoked when the
  command line parameter is not found in the ModeIn array.
  All output is sent to the current output device--usually the screen.
}

```
procedure Error;
begin
  writeln;
  writeln('An error has occurred. Please use only valid');
  writeln('DOS command names as parameters for HELP.');
  writeln('If you need help on how to use this program');
  writeln('just type, "HELP" by itself at the command');
  writeln('line and a help message will be printed.');
  Halt;
end;
```

{
  "ProgHelp" is a procedure that outputs text that guides the program's
  user. All output is sent to the current output device--usually the
  screen.
}

```
procedure ProgHelp;
begin
  writeln;
  writeln('HELP prints out help messages on some of the');
  writeln('more useful and popular DOS commands.');
  writeln('To use the utility just type HELP followed');
  writeln('by the name of the command that you want');
  writeln('help with.');
  writeln;
  writeln('Example: A>help dir');
  writeln;
  writeln('Help available for:');
  writeln;
  writeln('backup   chdir   cd       chkdsk   cls       comp');
  writeln('copy     date    del      dir      diskcomp  diskcopy');
  writeln('edlin    erase   find     format   graphics  mkdir');
  writeln('md       mode    more     path     print     prompt');
  writeln('rmdir    rd      rename   restore  sort      time');
  writeln('type     ver');
  Halt;
end;
```

{
"ParseCommandLine" is a procedure that checks if any data was i
at the DOS command line. If no data is there, then the "ProgHelp"
procedure is executed and the program is halted. Otherwise, the
HelpCode variable is set equal to the text on the command line.
}

```
procedure ParseCommandLine;
begin
  if ParamCount = 0
    then ProgHelp
    else
      begin
        HelpCode := ParamStr (1);
        HelpCode := UpItsCase (HelpCode);
      end;
end;
```

{
"Initialize" does exactly what the name implies. It is used in this
utility to intialize an array that is used in converting strings to
the defined scalar type, "ModeType."
}

```
procedure Initialize;
begin
  ModeIn[backupproc]    := 'BACKUP';
  ModeIn[chdirproc]     := 'CHDIR';
  ModeIn[cdproc]        := 'CD';
  ModeIn[chkdskproc]    := 'CHKDSK';
  ModeIn[clsproc]       := 'CLS';
  ModeIn[compproc]      := 'COMP';
  ModeIn[copyproc]      := 'COPY';
  ModeIn[dateproc]      := 'DATE';
  ModeIn[delproc]       := 'DEL';
  ModeIn[dirproc]       := 'DIR';
  ModeIn[diskcompproc]  := 'DISKCOMP';
  ModeIn[diskcopyproc]  := 'DISKCOPY';
  ModeIn[edlinproc]     := 'EDLIN';
  ModeIn[eraseproc]     := 'ERASE';
  ModeIn[findproc]      := 'FIND';
  ModeIn[formatproc]    := 'FORMAT';
  ModeIn[graphicsproc]  := 'GRAPHICS';
  ModeIn[mkdirproc]     := 'MKDIR';
  ModeIn[mdproc]        := 'MD';
  ModeIn[modeproc]      := 'MODE';
  ModeIn[moreproc]      := 'MORE';
  ModeIn[pathproc]      := 'PATH';
  ModeIn[printproc]     := 'PRINT';
  ModeIn[promptproc]    := 'PROMPT';
  ModeIn[rmdirproc]     := 'RMDIR';
  ModeIn[rdproc]        := 'RD';
  ModeIn[renameproc]    := 'RENAME';
```

(continued)

```
    ModeIn[restoreproc]    := 'RESTORE';
    ModeIn[sortproc]       := 'SORT';
    ModeIn[timeproc]       := 'TIME';
    ModeIn[typeproc]       := 'TYPE';
    ModeIn[verproc]        := 'VER';
    ModeIn[NotValid]       := 'NOTVALID';
  end;


{
  "ConvertToScalar" is the routine that does the actual
  conversion of a string to a defined scalar type, "ModeType."
}


procedure ConvertToScalar;
begin
  Found := False;
  Code := backupproc;
  repeat
    if ModeIn[Code] = HelpCode
      then Found := True
      else Code := Succ(Code);
  until Found or (Code = NotValid);
  if not Found
    then Error;
end;


{
  "_____PROCS" -- all the following procedures are used for writing
  help text on the screen. The five letters, "PROCS" were added to
  each procedure name to make sure that none of the name conflict
  with Turbo identifiers, procedures or functions.
}


procedure BACKUPPROCS;
begin
  writeln;
  writeln('BACKUP is used to make copies of the files on the');
  writeln('hard disk to floppy diskettes. It is more useful');
  writeln('than copying files to floppy because large files');
  writeln('can be broken into several files spread out over');
  writeln('several diskettes. The RESTORE command must be used');
  writeln('to get the files back.');
end;


procedure CHDIRPROCS;
begin
  writeln;
  writeln('CHDIR is used to change the current directory to');
  writeln('another. An abbreviation for the command is CD.');
  writeln('For example, to switch from the main directory');
```

```
    writeln('of drive C: to the subdirectory called "WP" you');
    writeln('type, "CD\WP."');
  end;

  procedure CDPROCS;
  begin
    CHDIRPROCS;
  end;

  procedure CHKDSKPROCS;
  begin
    writeln;
    writeln('CHKDSK is used to analyze your disk storage space');
    writeln('and to make sure that all the files are without');
    writeln('errors. It also displays information about the');
    writeln('computer"s memory. There are two parameters to');
    writeln('this command. One of them, "/V" will display a');
    writeln('list of all the files in all the directories of');
    writeln('the current drive. The other one, "/F" makes this');
    writeln('DOS command correct any errors it finds.');
  end;

  procedure CLSPROCS;
  begin
    writeln;
    writeln('CLS is used for clearing the screen.');
  end;

  procedure COMPPROCS;
  begin
    writeln;
    writeln('COMP compares two different files and reports');
    writeln('their differences. You must specify the names');
    writeln('of the two files either at the command line or');
    writeln('when the DOS command prompts you for it.');
  end;

  procedure COPYPROCS;
  begin
    writeln;
    writeln('COPY is used for moving files from directory to');
    writeln('directory and from diskette to diskette. This is');
    writeln('one of the most useful of the DOS commands. The');
    writeln('source name and destination name must be specified');
    writeln('at the command line. Either of these can contain a');
    writeln('drive letter and directory name.');
  end;
```

(continued)

```pascal
procedure DATEPROCS;
begin
  writeln;
  writeln('DATE is used for setting the system date. When');
  writeln('executed, it outputs its internal date which');
  writeln('is almost always wrong and prompts you for the');
  writeln('correct date.');
end;

procedure DELPROCS;
begin
  writeln;
  writeln('DEL is used for permanently purging your disk');
  writeln('of unwanted files. The name of the file that');
  writeln('you want to delete must follow the command.');
  writeln('This command works identically to the ERASE');
  writeln('command.');
end;

procedure DIRPROCS;
begin
  writeln;
  writeln('DIR displays a list of the files on your disk.');
  writeln('You can include a file name after the command');
  writeln('and DIR will search only for that file. If that');
  writeln('file name includes wildcard characters like "*"');
  writeln('or "?", then it scans for files that match your');
  writeln('template. For example, if you type "DIR *.COM"');
  writeln('then files ending in "COM" will be listed. There');
  writeln('are two parameters to this command, "/W" and');
  writeln('"/P." The "/W" displays the directory in a very');
  writeln('compact way across the screen. The "/P" forces');
  writeln('the directory command to pause after each');
  writeln('screenful.');
end;

procedure DISKCOMPPROCS;
begin
  writeln;
  writeln('DISKCOMP is a rarely used DOS command that');
  writeln('compares two diskettes and notifies you of');
  writeln('differences.');
end;

procedure DISKCOPYPROCS;
begin
  writeln;
  writeln('DISKCOPY is used for duplicating floppy');
  writeln('diskettes. Typically, it is used for');
  writeln('duplicating a diskette in drive A: to');
  writeln('drive B:. To accomplish this you would');
  writeln('type "DISKCOPY A: B:."');
end;
```

```
procedure EDLINPROCS;
begin
  writeln;
  writeln('EDLIN is the DOS line editor. It is used');
  writeln('for creating batch files and other small');
  writeln('text files.');
end;

procedure ERASEPROCS;
begin
  writeln;
  writeln('ERASE is used for permanently purging your disk');
  writeln('of unwanted files. The name of the file that');
  writeln('you want to delete must follow the command.');
  writeln('This command works identically to the DEL');
  writeln('command.');
end;

procedure FINDPROCS;
begin
  writeln;
  writeln('FIND is a command that can be used to search');
  writeln('a file for a specific series of characters.');
  writeln('It is known as a filter because it does not');
  writeln('directly work on a file. It takes its input');
  writeln('from the output of another program or from the');
  writeln('keyboard.');
end;

procedure FORMATPROCS;
begin
  writeln;
  writeln('FORMAT is used for preparing new diskettes for');
  writeln('use. It is usually followed by the drive letter');
  writeln('of the drive that contains the disk to be');
  writeln('formatted. The two most significant parameters');
  writeln('are "/V" and "/S." The "/V" means that you want');
  writeln('to specify a name for the disk. The "/S," that');
  writeln('you want to format a diskette with the system on');
  writeln('it (this makes the diskette bootable).');
end;

procedure GRAPHICSPROCS;
begin
  writeln;
  writeln('GRAPHICS is a memory resident program that allows');
  writeln('you to print the graphics screen to an IBM or EPSON');
  writeln('compatible printer. Once you execute this command,');
  writeln('you can press the SHIFT key and the PRTSC key and');
  writeln('your screen will be printed.');
end;
```

(continued)

```pascal
procedure MKDIRPROCS;
begin
  writeln;
  writeln('MKDIR is used for creating subdirectories on a');
  writeln('diskette.  An abbreviation for this command is');
  writeln('MD. For example, to make a directory called');
  writeln('"WP" you would type, "MD\WP."');
end;

procedure MDPROCS;
begin
  MKDIRPROCS;
end;

procedure MODEPROCS;
begin
  writeln;
  writeln('MODE is perhaps the most versatile DOS command.');
  writeln('It can be used to change video modes, set');
  writeln('the width of the printer, set the serial port');
  writeln('parameters, and redirect the printer to a serial');
  writeln('port.');
end;

procedure MOREPROCS;
begin
  writeln;
  writeln('MORE is a filter command much like the command');
  writeln('FIND. It is used when you want to see one screen');
  writeln('of text at a time.');
end;

procedure PATHPROCS;
begin
  writeln;
  writeln('PATH is a command that tells DOS where to look');
  writeln('for files when it is trying to execute a');
  writeln('command.  With the PATH command, you can make');
  writeln('DOS look in a specific subdirectory for your');
  writeln('programs.');
end;

procedure PRINTPROCS;
begin
  writeln;
  writeln('PRINT allows you to send out a preformatted');
  writeln('text file to the printer. It is memory resident');
  writeln('and can work in the background while you do');
  writeln('something else.  For example, if you want to');
  writeln('print out a file you would type, "PRINT file,"');
```

```
    writeln('where "file" is the name of what you want to');
    writeln('print.');
end;

procedure PROMPTPROCS;
begin
    writeln;
    writeln('PROMPT allows you to change the system prompt');
    writeln('from a drive letter to anything you prefer.');
    writeln('For example, if you type, "PROMPT At your command"');
    writeln('the new prompt will always say, "At your command."');
    writeln('Simply typing "PROMPT" at the command line,');
    writeln('will restore the original prompt.  A very useful');
    writeln('prompt is: "PROMPT $p$g." It will give you the');
    writeln('drive and path name of the current directory.');
end;

procedure RMDIRPROCS;
begin
    writeln;
    writeln('RMDIR removes subdirectories. An abbreviation');
    writeln('for this command is RD. To remove a directory');
    writeln('called "WP," you type "RD\WP."');
end;

procedure RDPROCS;
begin
    RMDIRPROCS;
end;

procedure RENAMEPROCS;
begin
    writeln;
    writeln('RENAME is used for changing the name of files.');
    writeln('You must specify the old name of the file and');
    writeln('the new name of the file. The two names must be');
    writeln('separated by a space.');
end;

procedure RESTOREPROCS;
begin
    writeln;
    writeln('RESTORE brings back files that were backed up');
    writeln('by the BACKUP command.');
end;

procedure SORTPROCS;
begin
    writeln;
    writeln('SORT is a filter command that will sort lines');
```

(continued)

```pascal
    writeln('in a text file. Since it is a filter, its input');
    writeln('must be the output of another file.');
end;


procedure TIMEPROCS;
begin
  writeln;
  writeln('TIME returns the current system time and prompts');
  writeln('you for the correct time. It is usually a good');
  writeln('idea to set the system date and time when you');
  writeln('start up the computer each time. If you do so,');
  writeln('your files will be saved with the right date and');
  writeln('time.');
end;


procedure TYPEPROCS;
begin
  writeln;
  writeln('TYPE is a DOS command used for displaying text');
  writeln('files on the screen. The format for its use is,');
  writeln('"TYPE filename.ext."');
end;


procedure VERPROCS;
begin
  writeln;
  writeln('VER returns the version number of DOS.');
end;


{
  "PrintHelpText" sends control to one of the procedures that
  prints out help depending on the command line parameter that
  the user types in.
}


procedure PrintHelpText;
begin
  case Code of
    backupproc    : BACKUPPROCS;
    chdirproc     : CHDIRPROCS;
    cdproc        : CDPROCS;
    chkdskproc    : CHKDSKPROCS;
    clsproc       : CLSPROCS;
    compproc      : COMPPROCS;
    copyproc      : COPYPROCS;
    dateproc      : DATEPROCS;
    delproc       : DELPROCS;
    dirproc       : DIRPROCS;
    diskcompproc  : DISKCOMPPROCS;
    diskcopyproc  : DISKCOPYPROCS;
    edlinproc     : EDLINPROCS;
    eraseproc     : ERASEPROCS;
```

```
      findproc      : FINDPROCS;
      formatproc    : FORMATPROCS;
      graphicsproc  : GRAPHICSPROCS;
      mkdirproc     : MKDIRPROCS;
      mdproc        : MDPROCS;
      modeproc      : MODEPROCS;
      moreproc      : MOREPROCS;
      pathproc      : PATHPROCS;
      printproc     : PRINTPROCS;
      promptproc    : PROMPTPROCS;
      rmdirproc     : RMDIRPROCS;
      rdproc        : RDPROCS;
      renameproc    : RENAMEPROCS;
      restoreproc   : RESTOREPROCS;
      sortproc      : SORTPROCS;
      timeproc      : TIMEPROCS;
      typeproc      : TYPEPROCS;
      verproc       : VERPROCS;
      NotValid      : Error;
    end;
  end;


begin   {Main Program}
  Initialize;
  ParseCommandLine;
  ConvertToScalar;
  PrintHelpText;
end.
```

KEYS

Type	External
Purpose	This program allows you to set the CAPS LOCK and NUM LOCK states.
Format	KEYS *or* KEYS state The term *state* can be any one of the following: capson capsoff numon numoff

Programs such as Lotus 1-2-3 and word-processing programs like WordStar or VolksWriter can be used with greater ease if a command like KEYS is used for setting the state of the CAPS LOCK and NUM LOCK keys. If you are a heavy Lotus user, you probably have already decided which state you like the NUM LOCK key to be in when you first start the program up. For some, having the key set to numbers is preferable, while for others the cursor control is more important. Whichever is the case, KEYS will allow you to set the keys quickly and effortlessly to either state before starting the program. Just include the command **KEYS numon** or **KEYS numoff** in a batch file that loads the program for you, and you will always have the numeric keypad set to your preference. You can also issue a command to have the CAPS LOCK key set to uppercase or lowercase depending on your preference in work sheets.

As mentioned, KEYS can also be used with word-processing programs. You would probably not want to have the CAPS LOCK key set, but you would almost definitely want the NUM LOCK key set to cursor control. In word processing you need to move around the document quickly, instead of entering numbers. To make the numeric keypad behave only as a cursor control pad at the time that you start a word-processing program, you would include the following in a batch file: **KEYS numoff**.

Typing KEYS by itself on the command line will return help on how to use the command.

Example 1—Getting help on the command

    A>keys
    help text is printed

Example 2—Batch file for Lotus 1-2-3 setting the numeric keypad for numbers

```
echo off
keys numon
lotus
```

Example 3—Batch file for Lotus 1-2-3 setting the numeric keypad for cursor control

```
echo off
keys numoff
lotus
```

Example 4—Batch file for WordStar setting the keyboard lowercase and the keypad to cursor control

```
echo off
keys capsoff
keys numoff
ws
```

Program

```
Program Keys;
{
        Title       : CAPS AND NUM SET     Version 1.00
        Author      : Robert Alonso
        Versions    : 1.00 January 12, 1986

        Purpose     : This program allows you to set the CAPS LOCK
                      and NUM LOCK state. This is useful if you
                      always prefer to enter a program like Lotus
                      1-2-3 with the numeric keypad always set to
                      numbers and not keys or vice a versa. Setting
                      the CAPS LOCK can also come in handy for
                      word processing programs.

        I/O Requirements : The program will work on IBM compatible
                      machines. Since it uses direct memory access,
                      it may not work on some machines that claim
                      to be compatible. However, it was tested on a
                      Corona PC (a machine that is often quirky) and
                      it worked fine.
}

type
  ModeType  = (capson,capsoff,numon,numoff,NotValid);
  MaxString = string[255];
```

(continued)

```
var
  Code        : ModeType;
  Mode        : string[8];
  ModeIn      : array [ModeType] of string[8];
  Found       : boolean;
  NumLock,
  CapsLock    : byte;
  MagicLocation : byte absolute $0040:$0017;
```

{
  "UpItsCase" is a function that takes a string of any length and
  sets all of the characters in the string to upper case. Its handy
  for comparing strings.
}

```
function UpItsCase (SourceStr : MaxString) : MaxString;
var
  I         : integer;

begin
  for I := 1 to length(SourceStr) do
    SourceStr[I] := UpCase(SourceStr[I]);
  UpItsCase := SourceStr
end;
```

{
  "Error" prints out a message when the input at the command
  line is unacceptable. In this program that occurs when the
  procedure "ConvertToScalar" does not find a valid match for
  the command line parameter in the ModeIn array.
}

```
procedure Error;
begin
  writeln;
  writeln('An error has occurred. Please make sure that');
  writeln('you use only valid input.');
  writeln;
  writeln('Example: A>keys capson');
  writeln;
  writeln('For help, just type "keys" at the command line.');
  Halt;
end;
```

{
  "Help" is a procedure that outputs text that guides the program's
  user. All output is sent to the current output device--usually the
  screen.
}

```
procedure Help;
begin
  writeln;
  writeln('KEYS will allow you to set the status of the');
  writeln('CAPSLOCK and NUMLOCK keys on your keyboard.');
  writeln('Although some keyboards have LEDs to indicate');
  writeln('the status, this program will not turn on or off');
  writeln('those LEDs. It will, however, set the desired');
  writeln('mode');
  writeln;
  writeln('Example : A>keys numon');
  writeln;
  writeln('Available modes:');
  writeln;
  writeln('capson  = all uppercase      capsoff = lowercase');
  writeln('numon   = numeric keys on    numoff  = cursor keys on');
  Halt;
end;

{
  "ParseCommandLine" is a procedure that checks if any data was input
  at the DOS command line. If no data is there, then the "Help"
  procedure is executed and the program is halted. Otherwise, the
  Mode variable is set equal to the text on the command line.
}

procedure ParseCommandLine;
begin
  if ParamCount = 0
    then Help
    else
      begin
        Mode := ParamStr (1);
        Mode := UpItsCase (Mode);
      end;
end;

{
  "Initialize" does exactly what the name implies. It is used in this
  utility to intialize an array that is used in converting strings to
  the defined scalar type, "ModeType."
}

procedure Initialize;
begin
  ModeIn[capson]   := 'CAPSON';
  ModeIn[capsoff]  := 'CAPSOFF';
  ModeIn[numon]    := 'NUMON';
  ModeIn[numoff]   := 'NUMOFF';
  ModeIn[NotValid] := 'NOTVALID';
  NumLock          := 32;
  CapsLock         := 64;
end;
```

(continued)

```
{
  "ConvertToScalar" is the routine that does the actual
  conversion of a string to a defined scalar type, "ModeType."
}

procedure ConvertToScalar;
begin
  Found := False;
  Code := capson;
  repeat
    if ModeIn[Code] = Mode
      then Found := True
      else Code := Succ(Code);
  until Found or (Code = NotValid);
  if not Found
    then Error;
end;


{
  "SetTheMode" does the work. All the other procedures are just used
  to either perform checks or conversions, but this is the meat of the
  program. Bits within the memory location called, "MagicLocation" are
  changed by this routine to get the desired results. The logical
  operators "AND" and "OR" are used to turn the bits on or off as
  required.
}

procedure SetTheMode;
begin
  case Code of
    capson   : MagicLocation := MagicLocation or CapsLock;
    capsoff  : MagicLocation := MagicLocation and (255 - CapsLock);
    numon    : MagicLocation := MagicLocation or NumLock;
    numoff   : MagicLocation := MagicLocation and (255 - NumLock);
    NotValid : Error;
  end;
end;


begin   {Main Program}
  ParseCommandLine;
  Initialize;
  ConvertToScalar;
  SetTheMode;
end.
```

LPRINT

Type   External

Purpose   This utility allows you to print out lines of text to any printer connected to your PC. It is useful for quickly typing out a mailing label or an address on an envelope.

Format   LPRINT
or
LPRINT any text that you want printed

Leading spaces are allowed. Just about anything that you can produce on the keyboard will be sent to the printer.

LPRINT lets you send any kind of text to a line printer connected to port 1 (LPT1). It is designed to fill the gap between using a word processor or a typewriter. It reads the command line as a string of characters and copies exactly what you type to the printer.

Example 1—Getting help on the command

```
A>lprint
```
help text is printed

Example 2—Printing out an address

```
A>lprint     Mary Doe
A>lprint     173 Any Street
A>lprint     Anyplace, XY 12345
```

Example 2 demonstrates the use of spaces to center the text to be printed.

Program

```
Program Lprint;
{
    Title       : LINE PRINTING PROGRAM    Version 2.00
    Author      : Robert Alonso
    Versions    : 1.00 September 27, 1985
                  2.00 October 7, 1985

    Purpose     : This program prints out a line of text
                  to the line printer.
```

(continued)

I/O Requirements : The program requires text input from the
                     command line of an MS-DOS or PC-DOS
                     computer. The line of text is then sent
                     to the line printer. Ideally, the printer
                     should be connected and on before executing
                     this program.
}

var
  CommandString : string[127] absolute cseg : $80;

                { An absolute string is used to extract the input
                  from the DOS command line because the Turbo Pascal
                  function ParamStr deletes extra spaces. Spaces
                  are valid input characters in Lprint. The command
                  line parameters always begin at offset $80. The
                  number stored at $80 is the length of the command
                  line and the string that follows is the actual
                  user input. }

{
  "Help" is a procedure that outputs text that guides the program's
  user. All output is to the current output device--usually the
  screen.
}

procedure Help;
begin
  writeln;
  writeln('LPRINT is used to output text to the printer.');
  writeln('You can use it by typing "lprint" at your DOS');
  writeln('prompt followed by the text that you want');
  writeln('printed. Example: A>lprint text to print');
  writeln;
  writeln('Turn on your printer before using this command.');
end;

{
  "GetCommandLine" is a procedure used for extracting the DOS command
  line argument. All input is from the absolute string CommandString.
}

procedure GetCommandLine;
begin
  if ParamCount = 0
    then
      begin
        Help; { If there has been no input, then user must not know how }
        Halt; { this program works. Display help text and stop execution. }
      end

```
      else
        begin
          delete (CommandString,1,1); { Get rid of first space which really }
        end;                          { isn't part of user input.            }
    end;


{
  "PrintCommandLine" is a procedure that prints the string variable
  CommandString after is has been processed by "GetCommandLine."
  All output is to the line printer, which should be connected to the
  computer and on.
}

procedure PrintCommandLine;
begin
  write (lst,CommandString);
end;


{
  "PrintCrLf" is a procedure that prints a carriage return and line feed.
  The output goes to the line printer.
}

procedure PrintCrLf;
begin
  writeln (lst);  { Most printers require that a carriage return be sent }
  end;            { before the text sent to it is printed.               }


begin    {Main Program}
  GetCommandLine;
  PrintCommandLine;
  PrintCrLf;
end.
```

CHAPTER 3

File Utilities

COUNT

Type	External
Purpose	This utility allows you to count the number of characters, words, and lines of text in an ASCII file. It is most useful to people who need to measure the quantity of text they are writing.
Format	COUNT or COUNT pathname filename.ext The *pathname* can be a drive letter and directory path such as b:\words\. The term *filename*.ext is the name of the text file that you want counted. If you choose a filename-extension that does not exist in the pathname that you specified, you will be told so.

COUNT is useful in any situation in which you must know how much you've written. If you are a student, you have probably been asked more than once and perhaps quite often to write a paper that's a few hundred or a thousand words. With this utility, you can be certain that you have written as many words as a professor has requested. But COUNT is not only for students. It can be used by anyone who does extensive text editing in their business. If you are a writer or editor, you can use it to make sure that you are writing text to fit the space in which it is going to be published.

Example 1—Getting help on the command
```
A>count
help text is printed
```

Example 2—Counting a text file

```
A>count sonnet.asc
Characters = 5768
Lines = 120
Words = 1345
```

Example 3—Attempting to count a file that does not exist

```
A>count nowords.txt
```

File does not exist in designated path

Program

```
Program Count;
{
    Title           : COUNT FILE CONTENTS      Version 2.00
    Author          : Robert Alonso
    Versions        : 1.00 October 1, 1985
                      2.00 October 8, 1985

    Purpose         : This program counts the number of characters
                      words and lines in a text file.

    I/O Requirements : The program will work on MS-DOS and PC-DOS
                       ASCII text files. It expects a file name with
                       optional drive specifier and path name in the
                       command line. Output consist of the results
                       of internal calculations on the contents of
                       the specified text file and is directed to the
                       screen.
}

const
  spcsym      = #32; { In ASCII, the space character is number 32, }
  lnefd       = #10; { the linefeed character is number 10, the    }
  crsym       = #13; { carriage return is number 13 and the tab    }
  tabsym      = #9;  { symbol is character number 9.               }

type
  Name        = string[128];

var
  letters     : integer; { The variables; "letters," "lines" and   }
  lines       : integer; { "words" are used in the counting        }
  words       : integer; { routines of the program.                }
  intext      : boolean; { "Intext" is either true or false.       }
  ch          : char;    { One character at a time is read from the}
  WorkName    : text;    { file. "WorkName" and "FileName" are     }
  FileName    : Name;    { used to designate the name of the file. }
```

(continued)

```
{
  "Exist" is a function that checks if a file exist in the designated
  drive and directory. It returns true or false.
}

function Exist (FileName : Name) : boolean;
var
   Fil       : text;

begin
   assign (Fil, FileName);
   {$I-} reset (Fil) {$I+};
   Exist := (IOresult = 0);
end;


{
  "Help" is a procedure that outputs text that guides the program's
  user. All output is sent to the current output device--usually the
  screen.
}

procedure Help;
begin
   writeln;
   writeln('COUNT will give you a fairly accurate estimate of');
   writeln('how many characters, words and lines are in your');
   writeln('text file. To use type: COUNT filename.ext');
end;


{
  "ParseCommandLine" is a procedure that checks if any data was input
  at the DOS command line. If no data is there, then the "Help"
  procedure is executed and the program is halted. Otherwise, the
  FileName variable is set equal to the text on the command line.
}

procedure ParseCommandLine;
begin
   if ParamCount = 0
      then
         begin
            Help;
            Halt;
         end
      else
         begin
            FileName := ParamStr (1);
         end;
end;
```

{
"SearchForFile" is a procedure that calls the "Exist" function to
check if a file exists. If it does not, a message is printed
and program execution is halted.
}

```
procedure SearchForFile;
begin
  if not Exist (FileName)
    then
      begin
        writeln;
        writeln('File does not exist in designated path.');
        Halt;
      end;
end;
```

{
"OpenFile" is a procedure that opens the file by the name,
"FileName." A drive and path can be included with the name.
}

```
procedure OpenFile;
begin
  assign (WorkName, FileName);
  reset (WorkName);
end;
```

{
"Initialize" is a procedure that sets all variables to their default
values.
}

```
procedure Initialize;
begin
  intext := false;
  letters := 0;
  lines := 0;
  words := 0;
end;
```

{
"CountCharacters" is a procedure that first gets characters from
the open file, "WorkName," amd then increments a counter to indicate
that another character has been read.
}

(continued)

```pascal
procedure CountCharacters;
begin
  read (WorkName, ch);
  letters := letters + 1;
end;
```

```
{
  "CountWords" is a procedure that counts the number of words
  in the file by checking for word delimeters. A space, line feed,
  tab or carriage return is usually a good indication of the end
  of a word.
}
```

```pascal
procedure CountWords;
begin
  if (ch = spcsym) or (ch = lnefd) or (ch = tabsym) or (ch = crsym)
    then intext := false
    else
      if not intext
        then
          begin
            intext := true;
            words := words + 1;
          end;
end;
```

```
{
  "CountLines" is a procedure that counts lines by checking the
  line feed characters in the file.
}
```

```pascal
procedure CountLines;
begin
  if ch = lnefd
    then lines := lines + 1;
end;
```

```
{
  "CloseFile" is a procedure that closes the file named, "WorkName."
}
```

```pascal
procedure CloseFile;
begin
  close (WorkName);
end;
```

```
{
  "OuputResults" is a procedure that outputs information to end user.
  The screen is used as the output device. The character count is
  incremented by 1 to conform with MS-DOS and PC-DOS which counts the
  EOF character in its file size count.
}

procedure OutputResults;
begin
  writeln;
  writeln('Characters = ',letters + 1);
  writeln('Lines = ',lines);
  writeln('Words = ',words);
end;


begin    {Main Program}
  ParseCommandLine;
  SearchForFile;
  OpenFile;
  Initialize;
     while not eof (WorkName) do
       begin

          CountCharacters;
          CountWords;
          CountLines;

       end; {While}

  CloseFile;
  OutputResults;
end.
```

CREATE

Type External

Purpose This utility greatly simplifies the creation of small to medium-sized text files. It can be used effectively for creating batch files.

Format CREATE
or
CREATE pathname filename.ext

The *pathname* can be a drive letter and directory path such as b: \fun \.
The term *filename*.ext is the name of the file and the extension that you wish to use. If you choose a filename-extension combination that is already in use in the pathname you specified, then CREATE will tell you that the file exists and that you should try another name. There is no need to worry about accidentally deleting a valuable file with this command.

Although DOS has two ways to create files, the EDLIN way and the COPY CON:filename.ext way, neither one is completely satisfactory, and one is even dangerous. CREATE is designed to give you a quick and responsive miniature word processor that you can use for creating text files. It does not have the frustrating tendencies of EDLIN—DOS' line editing program—or the danger inherent in copying keystrokes to a file through the COPY:CON method. CREATE works very similarly to the COPY:CON method of text entry but will never allow you to accidentally destroy an existing text file. With COPY:CON, any filename that you specify will be created. That means that any existing files with the same name are deleted and the new one is copied over it.

The most obvious use of CREATE is to type in batch files. Some of the batch files in other sections of this book can be typed in with CREATE. It will take any keystrokes that you give it and store them directly to disk in ASCII format—the most standard way of storing alphanumeric characters and the one DOS needs. Whenever you feel that you are finished, you simply press CONTROL Z or function key 6 and the file is stored to disk exactly as you typed it.

CREATE includes some editing features that you may find useful. They are primarily a result of using Turbo Pascal to develop these utilities. The backspace and delete keys can be used as well as ESC. Pressing ESC or CONTROL X will delete the text of the entire line that you are typing. To recall characters that were typed directly above in the previous line, you press CONTROL-D. In a similar fashion, pressing CONTROL-R will repeat all the characters in the previous line. Pressing RETURN or CONTROL-M will end the current line and place your cursor on the beginning of the next line.

If you ever need help recalling what the editing features are, you can simply type CREATE at the DOS prompt and a help screen will be printed explaining the details.

Example 1—Creating a file in current directory

```
A>create sample.txt
Pressing Control "Z" saves the file to disk:

----+----+----+----+----+----+----+----+----+----

This is a test of the CREATE command.
Type in several lines.
See, it really works!
```

Example 2—Creating a batch file in another drive

```
A>create b:autoexec.bat
Pressing Control "Z" saves the file to disk:

----+----+----+----+----+----+----+----+----+----

mode co80
ws
```

Example 3—Creating a file in another drive and subdirectory

```
A>create c:\lotus\bakgone.bat
Pressing Control "Z" saves the file to disk:

----+----+----+----+----+----+----+----+----+----

echo off
echo This file will delete all BAK files
echo in your LOTUS directory
pause
del c:\lotus\*.bak
echo on
```

Program

```
Program Create;
{
       Title       : TEXT FILE CREATOR      Version 2.00
       Author      : Robert Alonso
       Versions    : 1.00 September 30, 1985
                     2.00 October 7, 1985
```

(continued)

Purpose   : This program facilitates the creation of
                  small to medium size text files. It first
                  checks if the text file that you are trying
                  to create exists in the directory that you
                  specify. If the file already exists, the
                  program informs you and stops executing. It
                  is, thus, impossible to do damage to any
                  existing data.

  I/O Requirements : The program requires text input from the
                  console and also requires that a file name
                  with optional path name be specified in the
                  command line. Program is designed to work
                  under MS-DOS and PC-DOS. Keystrokes are
                  immediately output to the disk drive.
}

type
  Name   = string[128];

var
  Ch   : char; { "Ch" holds the keystroke on its way to the disk. }
  FileName   : Name;
  WorkName   : text;

{
  "Exist" is a function that checks if a file exist in the designated
  drive and directory. It returns true or false.
}

function Exist (FileName : Name) : boolean;
var
  Fil   : text;
begin
  assign (Fil, FileName);
  {$I-} reset (Fil) {$I+};
  Exist := (IOresult = 0);
end;

{
  "Help" is a procedure that outputs text that guides the program's
  user. All output is to the current output device--usually the
  screen.
}

procedure Help;
begin
  writeln;
  writeln ('CREATE is used for making small text files. For');
  writeln ('example, you can use it for typing in batch files.');
  writeln ('The advantage that "create" offers over the traditional');

```
  writeln ('COPY CON:filename.ext method is that it will not over-');
  writeln ('write an existing file. If a file already exists with');
  writeln ('the same file name, "create" will tell you so. Another');
  writeln ('advantage is that it is easier to use and remember.');
  writeln;
  writeln ('Example: CREATE filename.ext');
  writeln;
  writeln ('Editing commands: Backspace, Delete, Esc or CTRL-X for');
  writeln ('erasing all characters to beginning of current line,');
  writeln ('CTRL-D for recalling characters from previous line,');
  writeln ('CTRL-R for repeating all characters from previous line,');
  writeln ('Return or CTRL-M to end current line, and CTRL-Z to');
  writeln ('end all further input and save the file.');
end;


{
  "ParseCommandLine" is a procedure that checks if any data was input
  at the DOS command line. If no data is there, then the "Help"
  procedure is executed and the program is halted. Otherwise, the
  FileName variable is set equal to the text on the command line.
}

procedure ParseCommandLine;
begin
  if ParamCount = 0
    then
      begin
        Help;
        Halt;
      end
    else
      begin
        FileName := ParamStr (1);
      end;
end;


{
  "SearchForFile" is a procedure that calls the "Exist" function to
  check if a file exists. If it does, a warning message is printed
  and program execution is halted.
}

procedure SearchForFile;
begin
  if Exist (FileName)
    then
      begin
        writeln;
        writeln('File exists. Try another name.');
        Halt;
      end;
end;
```

(continued)

```
{
  "CreateFile" is a procedure that creates the file by the name,
  "FileName." A drive and path can be included with the name.
}

procedure CreateFile;
begin
  assign (WorkName, FileName);
  rewrite (WorkName);
end;


{
  "DisplayRuler" displays a ruler-like guide on the screen for
  text entry. It also gives instructions on how to save the file
  to disk.
}

procedure DisplayRuler;
begin
  writeln;
  writeln('      Pressing Control "Z" saves the file to disk.');
  write('----+----+----+----+----+----+----+----+');
  writeln('----+----+----+----+----');
end;


{
  "GetWriteCharacters" is a procedure that gets characters from the
  console device (the keyboard) and writes them to the disk in a
  text file format. The routine continues to get characters until an
  end-of-file (Control "Z") marker is retrieved from the console.
}

procedure GetWriteCharacters;
begin
  while not eof (con) do
    begin
      read (con,Ch);
      write (WorkName,Ch);
    end;
  close (WorkName);
end;


begin    {Main Program}
  ParseCommandLine;
  SearchForFile;
  CreateFile;
  DisplayRuler;
  GetWriteCharacters;
end.
```

DETAB

Type	External
Purpose	This utility removes TABS from text files. All occurrences of character number 9 (the tab symbol) are replaced with five spaces.
Format	DETAB *or* DETAB filename.ext detabfil.ext The term *filename.ext* can be any text file that contains TABS. The term *detabfil*.ext is an arbitrary name that you want to give the file without TABS.

Many word processors create text files that are full of TAB characters. You may even use the TAB key instead of typing five or eight spaces. Doing so makes sense for both you and the word processor. For a typist, it is easier to press TAB, and for the program it is more efficient to store a series of blanks as a TAB character. But some programs have trouble with TAB characters. One of these is Sidekick. When you load a text file into the Sidekick notepad, all TABS are represented as an uppercase letter I. Other editors that are used for programming also have this problem. For example, the Turbo Pascal editor does not like files with TABS in it either (it makes sense, since both Turbo Pascal and Sidekick are from Borland—it probably is the same editor code). DETAB can be used in instances where the program that you are using chokes on TABS. Just run the file through the DETAB program and out comes a file free from the annoying symbols.

You can change the number of spaces that DETAB substitutes for each TAB character by adding or deleting spaces from the commented line in the procedure called **ScanAndOutput**.

Example 1—Getting help on the command

```
A>detab
```
help text is printed

Example 2—Getting rid of TABS in a file called WORD.DOC and creating a file called WORD.TXT.

```
A>detab word.doc word.txt
```

Example 3—Same as Example 2, but WORD.DOC does not exist
    A>detab word.doc word.txt

The input file does not exist in the designated path.

Example 4—Same as Example 2, but WORD.TXT already exists
    A>detab word.doc word.txt

The output file already exists.

Program

```
Program Detab;
{
    Title       : REMOVE TABS          Version 1.00
    Author      : Robert Alonso
    Versions    : 1.00 February 5, 1986

    Purpose     : This program reads in a text file with
                  tabs and replaces each occurence with
                  five spaces.

    I/O Requirements : The program will work on MS-DOS and PC-DOS
                       ASCII text files. It expects an input file
                       name and output file name with optional drive
                       specifier and path name.
}
const
  tabsym      = #9;

type
  Name        = string[128];

var
  ch          : char;
  WorkNameIn,
  WorkNameOut : text;
  FileIn,
  FileOut     : Name;

{
 "Exist" is a function that checks if a file exist in the designated
 drive and directory. It returns true or false.
}

function Exist (FileName : Name) : boolean;
var
  Fil       : text;
```

```
begin
  assign (Fil, FileName);
  {$I-} reset (Fil) {$I+};
  Exist := (IOresult = 0);
end;
```

{
"Help" is a procedure that outputs text that guides the program's
user. All output is sent to the current output device--usually the
screen.
}

```
procedure Help;
begin
  writeln;
  writeln('DETAB is a program that removes tab symbols from');
  writeln('text files. This program is useful for those');
  writeln('editors that don"t handle tabs properly. DETAB will');
  writeln('scan your text file and replace each tab that it');
  writeln('finds with five spaces.');
  writeln;
  writeln('Example: A>detab wordproc.tab wordproc.dtb');
  Halt;
end;
```

{
"ParseCommandLine" is a procedure that checks if any data was input
at the DOS command line. If no data is there, then the "Help"
procedure is executed and the program is halted. Otherwise, the
FileIn and FileOut variables are equated to the text on the command line.
}

```
procedure ParseCommandLine;
begin
  if ParamCount = 0
    then Help
    else
      begin
        FileIn  := ParamStr (1);
        FileOut := ParamStr (2);
      end;
end;
```

{
"SearchForFile" is a procedure that calls the "Exist" function to
check if a file exists. If it does not, a message is printed
and program execution is halted.
}

(continued)

```pascal
procedure SearchForFile;
begin
  if not Exist (FileIn)
    then
      begin
        writeln;
        writeln('Input file does not exist in designated path.');
        Halt;
      end;
  if Exist (FileOut)
    then
      begin
        writeln;
        writeln('Output file already exists.');
        Halt;
      end;
end;
```

{
  "OpenFiles" is a procedure that opens the files that the program
  uses. Both input and output files are specified.
}

```pascal
procedure OpenFiles;
begin
  assign (WorkNameIn, FileIn);
  reset (WorkNameIn);
  assign (WorkNameOut, FileOut);
  rewrite (WorkNameOut);
end;
```

{
  "ScanAndOutput" reads in characters from the input file that
  contains tabs and then writes out the characters to the output
  file. All Tabs are converted to five spaces here. *Notice that
  any character could be checked for and replaced.*
}

```
procedure ScanAndOutput;
begin
  read (WorkNameIn, ch);
  if ch = tabsym
    then write (WorkNameOut,'     ')    { 5 spaces }
    else write (WorkNameOut,ch);
end;
```

{
  "CloseFiles" is a procedure that closes the file.
}

```
procedure CloseFiles;
begin
  close (WorkNameIn);
  close (WorkNameOut);
end;


begin     {Main Program}
  ParseCommandLine;
  SearchForFile;
  OpenFiles;
    while not eof (WorkNameIn) do
      begin
        ScanAndOutput;
      end; {While}
  CloseFiles;
end.
```

ENCODE

Type External

Purpose This utility allows you to make your text files and other files truly private: password encryption.

Format ENCODE
or
ENCODE filename.ext otherfil.ext password

The term *filename.ext* can be the name and extension of any file that you want encrypted, including worksheet files, database files, program files, and word processing files.
The term *otherfil.ext* is a name and extension that you give to the encoded copy of the original file.
The *password* is the text that you want the file to be encoded with. The password can be up to 128 characters long, but you must not include any spaces in it. For example, "mysecretpassword" is a valid password, but "my secret password" is not.

Most people have secret files that must be kept that way. Some of these files may contain clever algorithms used in a program that you don't want anyone to copy, or databases that contain information that you don't want other people to have, or for a corporate type; secret company strategies or personnel files. These files are usually safe only when locked up somewhere with a traditional lock and key. But with proper encryption, these files may be just as safe out in the open. You can run any type of file through this program and get what seems like gibberish on the other end. It would take a determined snoop a long time to figure out what the gibberish means, and chances are that the snoop might never find out.

ENCODE will take any file and scramble it with a password that you supply. And since this password can be as long as 128 characters, it is very difficult to decode the file (the longer the password, the tougher it is). To make it even tougher to crack, ENCODE scrambles the password that you provide before using it on the file. Without a copy of ENCODE, the would-be cracker must figure out what seemingly random bytes were used to encrypt the file. Using the ENCODE program, though, you can decode the file quickly by providing the correct password.

You must be very careful not to forget your password, because the file can't be decoded without it. Also, when you encrypt a file, you must remember to delete the original. ENCODE does not delete your original, because if some error occurred during the encryption process you would be left with a useless file. If you run

ENCODE on a file and the target file is created, you can delete the original without hesitation, though, because ENCODE is bug free. It is during the actual process of encrypting that a power failure or some other problem could be dangerous if the original file had been deleted by ENCODE.

Always test a file that you have decrypted before deleting the encrypted copy. You may have mistyped the password and further encrypted the file intead of decrypting it. If the file is alright, then delete the encoded version; otherwise, try again with the correct password.

Example 1—Getting help with the command
```
A>encode
help text is printed
```

Example 2—Encrypting a file called "report.doc" with "robert" as the password
```
A>encode report.doc report.enc robert
A>del report.doc    don't forget this
```

Example 3—Decrypting the file "report.enc" to "report.doc" with the password "robert."
```
A>encode report.enc report.doc robert
A>ws report.doc    always check before
A>del report.enc   deleting encrypted file
```

Example 4—Encrypting a program file
```
A>encode myprog.exe myprog.enc thisisthepassword
A>del myprog.exe
```

Example 5—Decrypting the program file
```
A>encode myprog.enc myprog.exe thisisthepassword
A>myprog     test it first
A>del myprog.enc
```

Example 6—Encrypting a Lotus 1-2-3 worksheet
```
A>encode sales.wks sales.enc chairman
A>del sales.wks
```

Example 7—Decrypting a Lotus 1-2-3 worksheet

    A>encode sales.enc sales.wks chairman
    A>lotus   *retrieve the file and test it*
    A>del sales.enc

Program

```
Program ENCODE;
{
    Title        : ENCODE          Version 1.00
    Author       : Robert Alonso
    Versions     : 1.00 February 11, 1986

    Purpose      : This program scrambles data or program files
                   so that they become completely hidden from
                   snoopers.

    I/O Requirements : The program will work on MS-DOS and PC-DOS
                       computers. It expects two file names followed by
                       a word that will be used for scrambling the
                       data. The specified file will be completely
                       encrypted to the new file.
}

const
  RecordSize    = 128;
  BufferSize    = 128;

type
  Name          = string[128];
  CodeString    = string[128];

var
  OldFile, NewFile      : File;
  FileIn, FileOut       : Name;
  Code                  : CodeString;
  Buffer                : array [1..RecordSize,1..BufferSize] of byte;
  RecsRead              : integer;


{
 "Exist" checks if a file exist in the designated drive and
 directory. It returns true or false.
}

function Exist (FileName : Name) : boolean;
var
   Fil        : text;
```

```pascal
begin
  assign (Fil, FileName);
  {$I-} reset (Fil) {$I+};
  Exist := (IOresult = 0);
end;
```

{
  "Error1" is a procedure that outputs text when the program's
  input is unacceptable. This procedure will be invoked when the
  input file that is specified in the command line parameter
  does not exist.
}

```pascal
procedure Error1;
begin
  writeln;
  writeln('Input file does not exist!');
  writeln;
  writeln('An error has occurred. Make sure that you have');
  writeln('typed in the name and path of the original file');
  writeln('correctly.');
  writeln;
  Halt;
end;
```

{
  "Error2" outputs text when the program's input is unacceptable.
  This procedure will be invoked when the output file that is
  specified in the command line parameter already exists.
}

```pascal
procedure Error2;
begin
  writeln;
  writeln('Output file already exists!');
  writeln;
  writeln('An error has occurred. Make sure that you have');
  writeln('typed in the name and path of the output file');
  writeln('correctly.');
  writeln;
  Halt;
end;
```

{
  "Help" is a procedure that outputs text that guides the program's
  user. All output is sent to the current output device--usually the
  screen.
}

(continued)

```pascal
procedure Help;
begin
  writeln;
  writeln('ENCODE scrambles any file into a completely unreadable');
  writeln('format. Care must be taken not to forget the code word');
  writeln('used for the encrypting, because you will not be able');
  writeln('to decrypt the file without it.');
  writeln;
  writeln('ENCODE will also unscramble a scrambled file. Just type');
  writeln('the file''s name followed by the output file name and the');
  writeln('code word in the exact sequence that you did to scramble it');
  writeln('and it will be restored.');
  writeln;
  writeln('Example: A>encode b:filename.ext b:otherfil.ext secretcode"');
  writeln;
  Halt;
end;


{
 "ParseCommandLine" checks if any data was input at the
 DOS command line. If all the data isn't there, then the "Help"
 procedure is executed and the program is halted. Otherwise,
 the FileIn variable is set equal to the first parameter on
 the command line, FileOut to the second and the variable
 Code is set equal to the third parameter on the command line.
}


procedure ParseCommandLine;
begin
  if ParamCount <> 3
    then Help
    else
      begin
        FileIn  := ParamStr (1);
        FileOut := ParamStr (2);
        Code    := ParamStr (3);
      end;
end;


{
 "EncodePassword" further protects a file from being decoded. When a
 a program such as this uses the exclusive or method, ASCII characters
 in the password that hit a space result in the letter of the password.
 This is, of course, unacceptable for security purposes. This procedure
 sets the high bit of the password or resets it if it is already set
 making it tougher to figure out the password from the encoded file.
 To further hinder any mild attemp at decoding the file a character 58
 is added to the password. When a character 58 hits a space character
 (32) it becomes an End-Of-File (EOF) character (26). When someone tries
 to see your file using DOS' "type" command, only a few nonsensical
 characters will be seen before the DOS prompt returns.
}
```

```
procedure EncodePassword;
var
  i   : byte;
  j,
  k   : integer;
  Ch  : char;

begin
  j := 128;
  for i := 1 to length (Code) do
    begin
      Ch := Code[i];             { Set the high bit of each character in the }
      k  := ord(Ch) xor j;       { password to provide extra protection.     }
      Code[i] := Chr(k);
    end;
  Code := Code + Chr(58);        { So that Exclusive Or in EncodeCharacters }
end;                             { gives an EOF (26) with a space (32).     }
```

{
  "SearchForFiles" is a procedure that calls the "Exist" function to
  check if the input file exists. If it does not, then the "Error1"
  procedure is invoked. Similarly, if the output file exists then
  the "Error2" procedure is invoked.
}

```
procedure SearchForFiles;
begin
  if not Exist(FileIn)
    then Error1;

  if Exist(FileOut)
    then Error2;
end;
```

{
  "OpenFiles" opens the input file and output file for
  the encoding.
}

```
procedure OpenFiles;
begin
  assign(OldFile, FileIn);
  reset(OldFile);
  assign(NewFile, FileOut);
  rewrite(NewFile);
end;
```

{
  "EncodeCharacters" performs the necessary work to scramble or
  descramble a file.
}

(continued)

```pascal
procedure EncodeCharacters;
var
  i,j,k,
  Ch     : byte;
  CodeCh : char;

begin
  i := length (Code);
  repeat
     BlockRead(OldFile,Buffer,BufferSize,RecsRead);

     for j := 1 to RecordSize do
       begin
         for k := 1 to BufferSize do
           begin
             CodeCh := Code[i];
             Buffer[j,k] := Buffer[j,k] xor ord(CodeCh);
             i := i - 1;
             if i = 0
                then i := length (Code);
           end;
       end;

     BlockWrite(NewFile,Buffer,RecsRead);

  until RecsRead = 0;
end;


{
  "CloseFiles" closes both the input and output file.
}

procedure CloseFiles;
begin
  close(OldFile);
  close(NewFile);
end;


begin    {Main Program}
  ParseCommandLine;
  SearchForFiles;
  EncodePassword;
  OpenFiles;
  EncodeCharacters;
  CloseFiles;
end.
```

LLIST

Type	External
Purpose	This utility allows you to print out files to the printer with proper page breaks and prevents sloppy printouts by avoiding the tear in computer paper.
Format	LLIST *or* LLIST myprog.pas The term *myprog.pas* can be a Turbo Pascal program listing or any other text file that you would like printed in a hurry.

DOS provides a very powerful command called PRINT that can be used to print files while you do something else with the computer. It is probably the only thing that the current DOS implementation can do concurrently with other programs. Unfortunately, though, PRINT only provides an elegant printout when another program has formatted the text for it. For example, a Lotus 1-2-3 print file (any file created from Lotus with the extension .PRN) can be printed using the PRINT command. But, what happens when you have a free-form text file on your disk—one that you need a quick printout for? Is it really necessary to load a 200K word processor just to reformat the text and print it out? Perhaps, but only if you need special effects such as underlining and boldface. For the quick and dirty printouts that still require some neatness, you can use LLIST.

LLIST was inspired by the BASIC command with the same name. Unlike its BASIC namesake, LLIST formats what it sends to the printer. Provided that you set the printhead to the beginning of a page before you begin, you will consistently obtain neat looking printouts that never come out on the perforation.

Example 1—Getting help on the command

    A>llist
    help text is printed

Example 2—Listing out a file called MYPROG.PAS to the printer

    A>llist myprog.pas

Program

```
Program Llist;
{
    Title       : LIST PROGRAM FILES     Version 1.00
    Author      : Robert Alonso
    Versions    : 1.00 May 5, 1985

    Purpose     : This program can be used for listing simple
                  text or program files to your printer.
                  Special codes to make your printer go into
                  bold, italic or condensed mode are not included
                  to make this program more universally useful.
                  However, you can use PMODE to set the printer's
                  mode before using this utility.

    I/O Requirements : The program will work on MS-DOS and PC-DOS
                  text files that can be typed to the screen. If
                  any strange characters are in the input file then
                  you will obtain unreliable results.
}

type
  Name       = string[128];

var
  WorkNameIn : text;
  FileIn     : Name;
  i,
  c          : byte;
  line       : string[132];

{
  "Error" is a procedure that outputs text when the program's
  input is unacceptable. This procedure will be invoked when the
  command line parameter is the name of a file that does not exist
  in the default or specified drive and directory.
}

procedure Error;
begin
  writeln;
  writeln('An error has occurred. You have asked this');
  writeln('program to print a file that does not exist.');
  writeln('Please locate the file and put the correct');
  writeln('drive and path as part of the command line.');
  Halt;
end;
```

{
  "Help" is a procedure that outputs text that guides the program's
  user. All output is sent to the current output device--usually the
  screen.
}

procedure Help;
begin
  writeln;
  writeln('LLIST can be used to list text files or program');
  writeln('source files--like Turbo Pascal or dBase III+');
  writeln('files. It is ideal for a programming environment');
  writeln('because you can quickly print out an old program');
  writeln('file for reference without having to load an editor');
  writeln('or even worse a word processor.');
  writeln;
  writeln('Example: A>llist exprog.pas');
  writeln;
  Halt;
end;

{
  "Exist" is a function that checks if a file exist in the designated
  drive and directory. It returns true or false.
}

function Exist (FileName : Name) : boolean;
var
  Fil   : text;

begin
  assign (Fil, FileName);
  {$I-} reset (Fil) {$I+};
  Exist := (IOresult = 0);
end;

{
  "ParseCommandLine" is a procedure that checks if any data was input
  at the DOS command line. If no data is there, then the "Help"
  procedure is executed and the program is halted. Otherwise, the
  FileIn variable is set equal to the text on the command line. In
  this version of the routine (it is used in many other programs
  in this book) a check is also made to see if the file exist. If
  it does not then the "Error" routine is executed and the program
  is halted.
}

(continued)

```
procedure ParseCommandLine;
begin
  if ParamCount = 0
    then Help
    else
      begin
        FileIn := ParamStr (1);
        if not Exist(FileIn)
          then Error;
      end;
end;
```

{
"OpenFile" is a procedure that opens the file that the program uses.
}

```
procedure OpenFile;
begin
  assign (WorkNameIn, FileIn);
  reset (WorkNameIn);
end;
```

{
"CloseFile" is a procedure that closes the file.
}

```
procedure CloseFile;
begin
  close (WorkNameIn);
end;
```

{
"DoIO" is the workhorse in this program. It maintains a count of how many lines have been printed and does line feeds to the appropriate spot on subsequent pages to maintain order. All significant input and output (not including "Help" and "Error") is performed within this routine. Lines are obtained from the input file and sent to the list device for printing.
}

```
procedure DoIO;
begin
 i := 4;
 for c := 1 to 2 do
   writeln(lst);    { Begin three lines from Top Of Form (TOF) }

  while not eof (WorkNameIn) do
   begin

   if i = 63
     then
       begin              { Keep three line top and bottom margin. }
        i := 3;           { I'm, of course, assuming a 66 line per }
        for c := 1 to 6 do   { page printer.                       }
          writeln(lst);
       end;
      readln(WorkNameIn, line);
      writeln(lst, line);     { Printer is used as an output text file. }
      i := i + 1;

    end; {While}
end;


begin  {Main}
 ParseCommandLine;
 OpenFile;
 DoIO;
 CloseFile;
end.
```

WSASCII

Type External

Purpose This utility converts WordStar document files to their ASCII counterparts. All nonprinting characters are removed.

Format WSASCII
or
WSASCII wordstar.doc filename.txt

Either parameter can include a drive name and path. For example, the command line could read as follows and still be valid:

A>wsascii b:report.doc c:\tc\upload.txt

Microsoft can't be faulted on this one. It can't possibly be expected to include a utility with DOS to convert the hieroglyphic output from a competitor's word processor. However, many computer owners either use or have used WordStar at one time. Just like popcorn is usually purchased with butter, computers are very often purchased with WordStar. Since WordStar is so omnipresent, a utility such as this can come in very handy when trying to convert the strange format to one that other word processors can understand. WSASCII does what its name implies; it converts Word-Star document files to ASCII—the accepted standard for text interchange. Once you convert a document to ASCII, it becomes much easier to import it into other programs and to telecommunicate it across the country to friends.

WSASCII by itself on the command line will print a help screen for the command.

Example 1—Getting help on the command

C>wsascii
help text is printed

Example 2—Converting a document to ASCII

C>wsascii c:paper.doc c:paper.asc

Example 3—Improper use of the command

C>wsascii c:document.doc
error message is printed

More than one filename must follow WSASCII—the original name of the file plus the name that you want given to the converted file.

Program

```
Program WSASCII;
{
    Title       : WORDSTAR TO ASCII    Version 1.00
    Author      : Robert Alonso
    Versions    : 1.00 February 9, 1986

    Purpose     : This program converts WordStar document files
                  into ASCII files that can be used for tele-
                  communications or for use with other word
                  processors.

    I/O Requirements : The program will work on MS-DOS and PC-DOS
                       WS document files. It expects two file names with
                       optional drive specifier and path name in the
                       command line. Output is sent to the second file
                       specified in the command line.
}

type
  Name      = string[128];
  ASCII     = set of 0..127;

var
  OldFile, NewFile           : text;
  FileName1, FileName2       : Name;
  AllChars, Exceptions, Print : ASCII;


{
  "Exist" checks if a file exist in the designated drive and
  directory. It returns true or false.
}

function Exist (FileName : Name) : boolean;
var
  Fil      : text;

begin
  assign (Fil, FileName);
  {$I-} reset (Fil) {$I+};
  Exist := (IOresult = 0);
end;


{
  "Error" is a procedure that outputs text when the program's
  input is unacceptable. This procedure will be invoked when the
  file that is specified in the command line parameter does not
  exist.
}
```

(continued)

```pascal
procedure Error;
begin
  writeln;
  writeln('File does not exist!');
  writeln;
  writeln('An error has occurred. Make sure that you have');
  writeln('typed in the name and path of the original file');
  writeln('correctly.');
  Halt;
end;
```

{
  "Help" is a procedure that outputs text that guides the program's
  user. All output is sent to the current output device--usually the
  screen.
}

```pascal
procedure Help;
begin
  writeln;
  writeln('WSASCII converts files created with WordStar to');
  writeln('a format that is easily transferred to other word');
  writeln('processors and other computers. The format is called');
  writeln('ASCII.');
  writeln;
  writeln('You must give this utility the name of the WordStar');
  writeln('file to be converted and the name of the file you');
  writeln('want it to create.');
  writeln;
  writeln('Example: A>wsascii c:\ws\report.doc c:ascii.txt"');
  writeln;
  writeln('The example converts "report.doc" in the "ws"');
  writeln('subdirectory to an ASCII text file called,');
  writeln('"ascii.txt" in the root directory.');
  Halt;
end;
```

{
  "ParseCommandLine" checks if any data was input at the DOS
  command line. If no data is there, then the "Help"
  procedure is executed and the program is halted. Otherwise, the
  FileName1 variable is set equal to the first parameter on
  the command line and the variable FileName2 is set equal
  to the second parameter on the command line.
}

```pascal
procedure ParseCommandLine;
begin
  if ParamCount <> 2
    then Help
    else
```

```
    begin
      FileName1 := ParamStr(1);
      FileName2 := ParamStr(2);
    end;
end;
```

{
"SearchForFile" is a procedure that calls the "Exist" function to
check if a file exists. If it does not, then the "Error" procedure
is invoked.
}

```
procedure SearchForFile;
begin
  if not Exist(FileName1)
    then Error;
end;
```

{
"Initialize" produces a set of characters that are deemed acceptable
to use by the procedure "ConvertCharacters."
}

```
procedure Initialize;
begin
  AllChars := [0..127];
  Exceptions := [0..8,11,12,14..31,127];
  Print := AllChars - Exceptions;
end;
```

{
"OpenFiles" opens the original WS document and a new
file for the ASCII conversion.
}

```
procedure OpenFiles;
begin
  assign(OldFile, FileName1);
  reset(OldFile);
  assign(NewFile, FileName2);
  rewrite(NewFile);
end;
```

{
"ConvertCharacters" performs the necessary stripping of the high bit
to get WordStar files to conform to the ASCII standard.
}

(continued)

```pascal
procedure ConvertCharacters;
var
  ch : char;
begin
  while not eof (OldFile) do
    begin
      read(OldFile,ch);
      ch := char(ord(ch) and 127);
      if ord(ch) in Print
        then write(NewFile,ch);
    end;
end;
```

{
"CloseFiles" closes both the original file and the newly created
file that contains the ASCII conversion.
}

```pascal
procedure CloseFiles;
begin
  close(OldFile);
  close(NewFile);
end;


begin     {Main Program}
  ParseCommandLine;
  SearchForFile;
  Initialize;
  OpenFiles;
  ConvertCharacters;
  CloseFiles;
end.
```

CHAPTER 4

System Utilities

ALTER

Type	External
Purpose	This utility allows you to alter the attribute byte of a file or subdirectory. With this utility you can hide a file or directory from normal DOS commands and even protect a file from being deleted.
Format	ALTER *or* ALTER filename.ext normal *or* ALTER filename.ext hidden *or* ALTER filename.ext protected *or* ALTER subdirect normal *or* ALTER subdirect hidden The term *filename.ext* can be any valid and existing filename and extension. The term *subdirect* can be any valid and existing subdirectory name.

Microsoft DOS version 3.0 (and those above 3.0) now comes with a command called ATTRIB.EXE that allows you to alter the read-only attribute bit, the bit that allows you to protect a file from modification and deletion. ALTER, similarly, allows you to modify this bit, but it does much more than just that. With ALTER, you can change a file's or subdirectory's status from normal to hidden and from hidden to normal, which is a handy feature to have around when you want to keep nosey people from looking at a file or even knowing that it exists at all. ALTER can be used by people with DOS 2.1 and above, thus making it more useful than the new ATTRIB command in DOS. A feature of ALTER that is worth mentioning is that it never actually changes the bit on the surface of the disk. ALTER calls an obscure internal DOS function called CHMOD (function 67) to do the changing, which is a plus because the dangerous part is performed by DOS, making it unlikely that any damage could befall one of your files. If you use ALTER to protect a file, you will notice that the file can't be deleted or modified afterwards. You might want to protect key files, like the executable portion of programs or important data.

ALTER by itself on the command line will print a help screen for the command.

Example 1—Getting help on the command
   C > alter
   help text is printed

Example 2—Protecting a file called "sample.txt."
   A > alter sample.txt protected

Example 3—Hiding a file
   A > alter sample.txt hidden

Example 4—Restoring a file to normal
   A > alter sample.txt normal

Example 5—Hiding a subdirectory
   C > alter lotus hidden

   The subdirectory called LOTUS would now be hidden.

Example 6—Restoring a subdirectory to normal
   C > alter lotus normal

Example 7—Protecting a subdirectory
   C > alter lotus protected

   An error message is printed because it is not necessary to protect a subdirectory.

Program

```
Program Alter;
{
    Title       : ATTRIBUTE CHANGER    Version 1.00
    Author      : Robert Alonso
    Versions    : 1.00 January 20, 1986

    Purpose     : This program allows you to change the
                  attribute of any file or subdirectory
                  on a DOS formatted diskette. A DOS function
                  call is used instead of a direct modify
                  to maintain compatibility with the majority
                  of DOS machines.

    I/O Requirements : The program will work on MS-DOS and PC-DOS
                       computers running DOS version 2.1 or greater.
}
type
  Name      = string[80];
  MaxString = string[255];
  AttribType = (Protected,Hidden,Normal,NotValid);
  RegRec    =
    record case integer of
      1: (AX, BX, CX, DX, BP, DI, SE, DS, ES, Flags : Integer);
      2: (AL, AH, BL, BH, CL, CH, DL, DH : Byte);
    end;

var
  Regs          : RegRec;
  AttribConv    : AttribType;
  DirectoryEntry : Name;
  Attribute     : string[9];
  AttribArray   : array [AttribType] of string[9];
  Value         : byte;
  CurrentAttrib : byte;
  Found         : boolean;


{
 "UpItsCase" is a function that takes a string of any length and
 sets all of the characters in the string to upper case. Its handy
 for comparing strings.
}

function UpItsCase (SourceStr : MaxString) : MaxString;
var
  I       : integer;

begin
  for I := 1 to length(SourceStr) do
    SourceStr[I] := UpCase(SourceStr[I]);
  UpItsCase := SourceStr
end;
```

(continued)

```
{
  "Error" outputs text when the program's input is unacceptable
  This procedure will be invoked when the command line parameters
  do not have the correct syntax.
}

procedure Error;
begin
  writeln;
  writeln('The requested directory entry may not exist.');
  writeln('You may also be getting this error message if');
  writeln('you have not typed in the allowed attribute');
  writeln('choice correctly.');
  writeln;
  writeln('Acceptable attributes: Protected, Hidden, Normal');
  Halt;
end;


{
  "Help" is a procedure that outputs text that guides the program's
  user. All output is sent to the current output device--usually the
  screen.
}

procedure Help;
begin
  writeln;
  writeln('ALTER can be used to change the attribute of');
  writeln('either files or subdirectories. You can use this');
  writeln('utility to hide sensitive files or protect');
  writeln('important files from being changed or deleted.');
  writeln('Example: A>ALTER filename.ext hidden');
  writeln;
  writeln('The allowed attributes are: Protected, Hidden');
  writeln('and Normal.');
  Halt;
end;


{
  "SubMessage" prints a message about subdirectories if the user tries
  to protect a subdirectory.
}

procedure SubMessage;
begin
  writeln;
  writeln('It is not necessary to protect subdirectories. They are');
  writeln('automatically protected by DOS. For example, you can"t remove');
  writeln('a subdirectory unless every file in it has already been deleted.');
  Halt;
end;
```

{
  "Initialize" is used to make sure that the temporary values for the
  MS-DOS registers are zero. It also initializes the array, "AttribArray."
}

```
procedure Initialize;
begin
  FillChar( Regs,SizeOf(Regs),0 ); {Init the registers}
  AttribArray[Protected] := 'PROTECTED';
  AttribArray[Hidden]    := 'HIDDEN';
  AttribArray[Normal]    := 'NORMAL';
  AttribArray[NotValid]  := 'NOTVALID';
end;
```

{
  "ParseCommandLine" is a procedure that checks if any data was input
  at the DOS command line. If no data is there, then the "Help"
  procedure is executed and the program is halted. Otherwise, the
  "DirectoryEntry" and "Attribute" variables are set equal to the command
  line parameters.
}

```
procedure ParseCommandLine;
begin
  if ParamCount = 0
    then Help
    else
      begin
        DirectoryEntry := ParamStr (1);
        Attribute      := UpItsCase(ParamStr (2));
      end;
end;
```

{
  "Convert_To_Scalar" converts the command line parameters to
  scalar format. This is needed to use the command line strings
  in a case statement.
}

```
procedure Convert_To_Scalar;
begin
  Found := False;
  AttribConv := Protected;
  repeat
    if AttribArray[AttribConv] = Attribute
      then Found := True
      else AttribConv := Succ(AttribConv);
  until Found or (AttribConv = NotValid);
  if not Found
```

(continued)

```pascal
      then Error;
end;


{
  "ExtractAttributeValue" is used for changing a scalar value produced in
  the previous routine to a numeric value. The numeric value is used for
  changing the attribute of a file or directory.
}


procedure ExtractAttributeValue;
begin
  case AttribConv of
    Protected : Value :=   1;
    Hidden    : Value :=   6;
    Normal    : Value := 248;  { get rid of bits 0-2. }
    NotValid  : Error;
  end;
end;


{
  "CallChmod" calls the internal DOS function number 67 to modify
  the attribute of a file or directory. All of the work is performed
  in this routine. The registers are set and then a call is made to
  MsDos interrupt 21.
}


procedure CallChmod;
var i : integer;
begin
  DirectoryEntry := UpItsCase(DirectoryEntry) + chr(0);
  Regs.DS  := Seg(DirectoryEntry);
  Regs.DX  := Ofs(DirectoryEntry) + 1;
  Regs.AH  := 67;   { AH is set to 67 for the function call. }
  Regs.AL  := 0;    { if AL := 0 then attribute is returned in CL. }
  MsDos(Regs);      { Get the current attribute. }
  CurrentAttrib := Regs.CL;

  if (CurrentAttrib = 0) or (CurrentAttrib = 2) or (CurrentAttrib = 3)
    then Error;

  if (CurrentAttrib and 16 = 16) and (Value = 1)
    then SubMessage;
```

```
    if (CurrentAttrib = 22) and (Value = 248) {special for hidden subdirectories}
      then Value := CurrentAttrib and 232
      else if (CurrentAttrib = 16) and (Value = 6) {special for subdirectories}
          then Value := 6
          else if Value = 248
              then Value := CurrentAttrib and Value
              else Value := CurrentAttrib or Value;

  Regs.DS := Seg(DirectoryEntry);
  Regs.DX := Ofs(DirectoryEntry) + 1;
  Regs.CX := Value;
  Regs.AH := 67;   { AH is set to 67 for the function call.   }
  Regs.AL := 1;    { if AL := 1 then attribute in CL is set.  }
  MsDos(Regs);     { Change the attribute.                    }
end;


begin       {Main Program}
  Initialize;
  ParseCommandLine;
  Convert_To_Scalar;
  ExtractAttributeValue;
  CallChmod
end.
```

DIAG

Type   External

Purpose   This program diagnoses your PC. It displays the amount of memory, the disk drives, the type of video output that you are using, and other pertinent information about your system, including a performance analysis.

Format   DIAG

This utility is more for fun than for anything else. It does have some practical applications, however. If you are considering buying a new computer or are evaluating a computer for any reason, this program will give you a rough performance analysis of the machine compared to a plain vanilla IBM PC, and it will also tell you some interesting facts. You will be able to find out who owns the copyright to the ROM BIOS chip in the PC as well as the one that manages the hard drive; the date that the BIOS was last revised; whether the machine's ID byte designates it as a JR, PC, XT, AT, Convertible, or Compaq; and also a number of other facts about the machine.

Trying this program on some of the Turbo boards for a PC can yield interesting results. You might be able to test if there is any discernible improvement in speed measured by using the performance index. Another interesting test is to see if the NEC V-20 processor actually speeds up the PC by 20 percent (hard to believe).

DIAG doesn't print help or error messages, because it requires no user input and works without any intervention. The greatest utility that this program has is the program source code that follows. Using some or all of the routines that are included in DIAG, you can write self-installing programs that automatically "know" what machine they are running on and under what type of video mode. With the routines provided, you could write a program that could adjust the width of its screen output if the user is in 40-column mode or switch from color to mono or vice versa depending on the settings that these procedures return. You would even be able to find out specifically which machine the program is running on by keeping a table of copyright messages that the **Copyright** procedure is likely to run across.

Example 1—Getting your PC diagnosed

```
A>diag
```
complete diagnosis follows

Program

```
Program Diag;
{
    Title      : SYSTEM INFORMATION    Version 2.00
    Author     : Robert Alonso
    Versions   : 1.00 May 12, 1986
                 2.00 October 22, 1986

    Purpose    : This program checks several things about
                 your PC. ROM memory locations as well as
                 interrupt calls are made to get the required
                 data. The accuracy of the procedures is fairly
                 high, but not infallible. Depending on how
                 compatible your system is, some of the results
                 could be slightly off. For example, the ROM Date
                 and ROM Copyright routines may fail to find
                 anything meaningful in your machine. Typically,
                 though, these two routines will find something.

    I/O Requirements : The program will work on IBM compatible PCs that
                       are running a version of MS-DOS or PC-DOS.
}

type
  RegRec   =
    record case integer of
      1: (AX, BX, CX, DX, BP, DI, SE, DS, ES, Flags : Integer);
      2: (AL, AH, BL, BH, CL, CH, DL, DH : Byte);
    end;

  ASCII    = set of 0..127;
  string4  = string[4];

var
  Regs        : RegRec;
  bit         : array[0..15] of boolean;
  AllChars,
  Exceptions,
  Print       : ASCII;

procedure Initialize;
begin
  AllChars   := [0..127];
  Exceptions := [0..8,11,12,14..31,43,46,127];
  Print      := AllChars - Exceptions;
end;

{
  "RomDate" scans an area of the ROM BIOS chip for a date stamp.
  This date stamp is in ASCII characters and is thus very easy to
  get and output to the screen. Some systems may not have the
  date stamp.
}
```

(continued)

```pascal
procedure RomDate;
type
  datemem = array [0..7] of char;

var
  date : datemem absolute $F000:$FFF5;
  i    : byte;

begin
  write('ROM BIOS Date           : ');
  for i := 0 to 7 do write(date[i]);
end;


{
  "Copyright" scans the entire BIOS or Fixed Disk ROM area for the letters,
  "Cop" which are found in the word, "Copyright" or "Copr." This is done
  to find out who wrote the BIOS and FD ROM. The BIOS copyright owner typically
  is the manufacturer of the PC.
}

procedure Copyright (WhichROM : string4);
type
  ROMchip = array [1..8092] of byte;

var
  BIOS  : ROMchip absolute $FE00:$0000;
  FD    : ROMchip absolute $C800:$0000;
  ROM   : ROMchip;
  i,
  j     : integer;
  temp1,
  temp2,
  temp3 : byte;

begin
  writeln;
  i := 0;
  j := 0;
  if WhichROM = 'BIOS'
    then
      begin
        ROM := BIOS;
        write('ROM BIOS Identification : ');
      end
    else
      begin
        ROM := FD;
        write('Fixed Disk ROM Id       : ');
      end;
  if ((ROM[i+1] = $55) and (ROM[i+2] = $AA)) or (WhichROM = 'BIOS')
    then
      begin
        repeat      {Search for 'Cop'}
```

```
            i := i + 1;
            temp1 := ROM[i];
            temp2 := ROM[i + 1];
            temp3 := ROM[i + 2];
            if (temp1 = ord('C')) or (temp1 = ord('c'))
              then                { Done this way to speed up search. }
                begin
                  if (temp2 = ord('O')) or (temp2 = ord('o'))
                    then              { If first condition is not met,  }
                      begin
                        if (temp3 = ord('P')) or (temp3 = ord('p'))
                          then       { others are not tested.           }
                            begin

                              repeat    { Skip string, "Copyright"      }
                                i := i + 1;
                              until ROM[i] = 32;

                              repeat    { Skip spaces, find first character. }
                                i := i + 1;
                              until ROM[i] <> 32;

                              j := i;
                              while ROM[j] in Print do  { Print out meaningful }
                                begin                   { charaters.           }
                                  write(chr(ROM[j]));
                                  j := j + 1;
                                end;

                              if ROM[j] = 46
                                then write('.');
                            end;
                      end;
                end;
            until (i = 8089) or (j <> 0);
            if j = 0
              then write('Nothing meaningful found');
          end
        else write('ROM not present');
end;


{
  "MachineType" scans a byte in the ROM BIOS that can be accurately used
  to find out what type of IBM machine the program is running on. It can
  also be used for the Compaqs and Corona. Possibly others as well.
}

procedure MachineType;
var
  MachineID : byte absolute $F000:$FFFE;

begin
  write('Machine ID        : ');
  case MachineID of
```

(continued)

```
      255  : writeln('PC');
      254  : writeln('XT, Portable PC or Corona');
      253  : writeln('PCjr');
      252  : writeln('AT');
      251  : writeln('IBM XT/Enhanced Keyboard');
      249  : writeln('IBM Convertible');
      154  : writeln('Compaq Plus');
       45  : writeln('Compaq');
    else     writeln(MachineID);
    end;
end;

{
  "DiskDrives" reports how many disk drives are connected to the machine.
  This number is obtained from the interrupt call performed in the procedure
  called, "CheckEquipmentList."
}

procedure DiskDrives;
var
  temp : byte;

begin
  if bit[0]
    then
      begin
        temp := Regs.AL and 192;
        write('Floppy Drives          : ');
        case temp of
          192 : writeln('4');
          128 : writeln('3');
           64 : writeln('2');
            0 : writeln('1');
        end;
      end;
end;


{
  "Printers reports the number of printer ports that are connected to the
  machine. This number is also obtained from the interrupt call in the
  procedure called, "GetEquipmentList."
}

procedure Printers;
var
  temp : byte;

begin
  temp := Regs.AH and 192;
  temp := temp shr 6;
  writeln('Printer Ports          : ',temp);
end;
```

{
"SerialPorts" reports the number of serial ports that are connected
to the machine. The information is obtained from an interrupt call that
takes place in the procedure "GetEquipmentList."
}

```
procedure SerialPorts;
var
  temp : byte;

begin
  temp := Regs.AH and 14;
  temp := temp shr 1;
  writeln('Serial Ports          : ',temp);
end;
```

{
"GameAdapter" checks to see if a game adapter is connected to your machine.
The procedure actually checks the Bit array to see if the appropriate
bit is TRUE. The interrupt call in procedure "GetEquipmentList" stores
the data in the Bit array for this procedure and others to use it.
}

```
procedure GameAdapter;
begin
  write('Game Adapter         : ');
  if bit[12]
    then writeln('Installed')
    else writeln('Not present');
end;
```

{
"VideoMode" uses bits from the call in "GetEquipmentList" to determine
the current video mode.
}

```
procedure VideoMode;
var
  temp : byte;

begin
  temp := Regs.AL and 48;
  write('Video Mode           : ');
  case temp of
    48  : writeln('80 MONO');
    32  : writeln('80 COLOR');
    16  : writeln('40 COLOR');
  end;
end;
```

(continued)

{
"DOSversion" uses a DOS function to determine which version of
DOS this program is running under. A trivial piece of code as you
can see.
}

procedure DOSversion;
var
  temp : real;

begin
  Regs.AH := 48;
  MsDos(Regs);
  temp := Regs.AL + (Regs.AH/100);
  writeln('DOS Version   : ',temp:4:2);
end;

{
"PerformanceIndex" generates a number from which the machine that
is running this program can be judged. An IBM PC (since it is the
de facto standard) is used as the standard and gets a 1.0 in the
index. Machines that are twice as fast or have co-processor chips
will have larger indexes. An index of 2.0 will be exactly twice as
fast as the IBM PC.
}

procedure PerformanceIndex;   { Relative to IBM PC }
var
  temp   : string[8];
  i,
  oldlength   : integer;
  Index,
  x,y,z   : real;
  Seconds,
  Hundred,
  DifSeconds : byte;
  DifHundred : real;

begin
  Regs.AH := $2C;
  MsDos(Regs);
  Seconds := Regs.DH;
  Hundred := Regs.DL;
writeln;
write('Performance Index   : ');
x := 5;
y := 7;
z := 5;
for i := 1 to 250 do
  begin

```
      x := y * z;                   { Numerical processes are performed }
      x := y / z;
      x := y + z;
      x := y - z;
      str(x,temp);
      oldlength := length(temp);    { As well as string processes to   }
      temp := temp + temp;          { test the performance of the      }
      temp := copy(temp,1,oldlength); { machine.                       }
    end;
  Regs.AH := $2C;
  MsDos(Regs);
  if Seconds > Regs.DH
    then Regs.DH := Regs.DH + 60;
  DifSeconds := Regs.DH - Seconds;
  DifHundred := Regs.DL - Hundred;
  Index := 164 / ((DifSeconds * 100) + DifHundred);  {164 is an IBM PC}
  write(index:3:1);
  writeln;
end;
```

{
  "CheckMemorySize" uses an interrupt call to obtain the amount of
  memory in use by the system. The information that this returns is
  usually identical to the system board switch settings. Therefore,
  expanded memory boards like the Intel Aboveboard will not be taken
  into account by this procedure. "EmsCheck," however, will indicate
  the amount of expanded memory that is available.
}

```
procedure CheckMemorySize;
var
  temp : integer;

begin
  intr(18,Regs);
  temp := Regs.AX;
  writeln('Memory              : ',temp,'K');
end;
```

{
  "EmsCheck" is used for checking the presence of Microsoft expanded
  memory. This routine gets the address that interrupt $67 points to
  and then scans that area for the sequence of characters, "EMMXXX0"
  which is present if LIM memory is being used. A check is then made
  to figure out the total amount of LIM memory that is present.
}

```
procedure EmsCheck;
var
  i,
  Segment,
  Offset : integer;
```

(continued)

```pascal
      letter  : char;
      name    : string[8];
      manager : file;

  begin
      write('Expanded Memory         : ');
      Regs.AH := $35;
      Regs.AL := $67;
      MsDos(Regs);
      Segment := Regs.ES;
      Offset := 9;
      for i := 0 to 8
        do
          begin
            letter := chr(mem[Segment:Offset+i]);
            name[i] := letter;
          end;
      name[0] := #8;
      if name = 'EMMXXXX0'
        then
          begin
            Regs.AH := $42;         { EMM Function 3: Get number of pages. }
            Intr($67,Regs);
            i := Regs.DX * 16;      { number of pages times 16K.           }
            writeln(i,'K');
          end
        else writeln('Not present');
  end;


  {
    "CheckEquipmentList" is one of the workhorses of this program. Many
    of the other procedures depend on this one for their raw data. An
    interrupt is executed to obtain a two byte bit encoded list of the
    equipment on the PC (Please see an IBM Technical Reference Guide for
    further study). An array called Bit is set up by this procedure so
    that other procedures can quickly obtain information about the
    equipment bytes in bit format.
  }

  procedure CheckEquipmentList;
  var
    i,
    temp : byte;
```

```
begin
  intr(17,Regs);
  for i := 0 to 15 do
    begin
      temp := Regs.AX shr i;
      if odd(temp)
        then bit[i] := TRUE
        else bit[i] := FALSE;
    end;
end;

{
  "PrintHeading" simply prints out a copyright message and
  two lines of help.
}

procedure PrintHeading;
begin
  writeln;
  writeln('Diag - Version 2.00, (C) Copr 1986, Robert Alonso');
  writeln;
  writeln('Performance index is relative to IBM PC. A result greater');
  writeln('than 1.0 means that the machine is faster.');
  writeln;
end;

begin  {Main Program}
  Initialize;
  PrintHeading;
  DOSversion;
  CheckMemorySize;
  EmsCheck;
  CheckEquipmentList;
  DiskDrives;
  Printers;
  SerialPorts;
  VideoMode;
  GameAdapter;
  MachineType;
  RomDate;
  Copyright('BIOS');
  Copyright('FD');
  PerformanceIndex;
end.
```

DISECT

Type   External

Purpose   This utility allows the reading and writing of absolute disk sectors. With this utility you can change the directory and modify the attribute byte of a file or patch any software package directly on the disk.

Format   DISECT

DISECT is a very powerful utility that can also be very dangerous. This warning comes first for a good reason: With DISECT you can modify anything that you want on the surface of the disk. It bypasses DOS altogether, which means that you really have nothing to stop you. This facility is great if you are experienced and need to change a byte on the disk as quickly as possible but can be extremely dangerous for an inexperienced tinkerer. So be careful!

With that out of the way, you are now entitled to a brief explanation of what you can do with DISECT. Let's say that you have a program, such as COPY IIPC, that you use all the time but do not want anyone to know you are using. Well, if you have tried to be discreet about your use of COPY IIPC, you know that it is next to impossible. It prints an entire screen of gibberish before it even starts to make your archival copy. The gibberish is really not necessary. With DISECT, you can find where the message begins on the disk and write a $ symbol there. Every time that you load COPY IIPC after that, it will never print the message. (The $ symbol is used by a print string routine in DOS to mark the end of the string. Placing it at the beginning would prevent any portion of the string from being printed.)

The miraculous things that you can do with DISECT are limited only by your imagination. For example, how about putting in lowercase letters in a volume name. DISECT can be used to locate the current diskette volume name and change it. You could have a volume label containing the string **R.Alonso**. But you probably would substitute your name, of course.

Example 1—Using DISECT on your PC

    A>disect
    program prompts you

Example 2—Trying to DISECT a disk that's not there

    A>disect
    answer prompts and no disk present
    error message printed

Program

```
Program Disect;
{
    Title       : DISK SECTOR EDITOR      Version 2.00
    Author      : Robert Alonso
    Versions    : 1.00 September 28, 1985
                  2.00 May 13, 1986

    Purpose     : This program can be used to edit the contents
                  of disk sectors or just inspect them to see
                  what they hold. This program bypasses DOS for
                  the read and write to the diskette so care should
                  be excercised in using it. While developing it, I
                  accidentally changed a couple of bytes in the
                  sector that holds the FAT and wound up with an
                  unusable diskette. Fortunately, it was a floppy
                  and I had something that approximated a backup.
                  Because of this experience, I have intentionally
                  limited the use of this program on floppies. You
                  can, however, make it work with a hard drives by
                  deleting the check that is made in the procedure
                  AskForInput. Although the program was crippled, it
                  does have the capability in the current code.

    I/O Requirements : The program will work on IBM compatible machines.
                  If you decide to make this program work with hard
                  disks you should make sure that your drive is fairly
                  compatible. One good way of knowing how compatible
                  the drive is, is to check if you need a software
                  driver to make it work with your machine. If you
                  don't need extra software then you should be OK.
}
type
  SectorType = array [0..511] of byte;

  RegRec   =
    record case integer of
      1: (AX, BX, CX, DX, BP, DI, SE, DS, ES, Flags : Integer);
      2: (AL, AH, BL, BH, CL, CH, DL, DH : Byte);
    end;

  HexStr   = string[2];

var
  SectorBuffer : SectorType;
  Regs         : RegRec;
  DriveNumber,
  TrackNumber,
  HeadNumber,
  SectorNumber : integer;
  Answer       : string[3];
  By,
  NewValue     : integer;
  Continue     : boolean;
```

(continued)

```
{
    "SectorRead" read a sector into the buffer by using a ROM BIOS
    interrupt. All preparations for the call to the BIOS are done
    by setting the appropriate registers.
}

function SectorRead (

        var
          DriveNumber  : integer;
          TrackNumber  : integer;
          HeadNumber   : integer;
          SectorNumber : integer ) : byte;  {status code returned}

begin
  Regs.ES := Seg(SectorBuffer);
  Regs.BX := Ofs(SectorBuffer);
  Regs.CH := TrackNumber;
  Regs.CL := SectorNumber;
  Regs.DH := HeadNumber;
  Regs.DL := DriveNumber;
  Regs.AH := 2;  {read a sector}
  Regs.AL := 1;
  Intr (19,Regs);          {Rom-Bios service - Hex 13}
  SectorRead := Regs.AH;
end;


{
    "SectorWrite" writes a sector into the buffer by using a ROM BIOS
    interrupt. All preparations for the call to the BIOS are done
    by setting the appropriate registers. The only difference between this
    function and "SectorRead" is that the AH register is set to a 3
    instead of a 2. These two could be made one and a parameter fed to it
    that tells it wether it is a read or write. For the purpose of clarity,
    they have been separated here.
}


function SectorWrite (

        var
          DriveNumber  : integer;
          TrackNumber  : integer;
          HeadNumber   : integer;
          SectorNumber : integer ) : byte;  {status code returned}

begin
  Regs.ES := Seg(SectorBuffer);
  Regs.BX := Ofs(SectorBuffer);
  Regs.CH := TrackNumber;
  Regs.CL := SectorNumber;
  Regs.DH := HeadNumber;
  Regs.DL := DriveNumber;
```

```
    Regs.AH := 3;  {write a sector}
    Regs.AL := 1;
    Intr (19,Regs);            {Rom-Bios service - Hex 13}
    SectorWrite := Regs.AH;
end;
```

{
  "Hex" takes a byte and converts it to a hexadecimal representation.
  This function is used by the program for output of neat numbers in
  the display screen.
}

```
function hex (decimalvalue : byte) : HexStr;
const
  map : array [0..15] of char = '0123456789ABCDEF';

var
  tmp : HexStr;

begin
  tmp[2] := map[(decimalvalue mod 16)];
  tmp[1] := map[(decimalvalue div 16)];
  tmp[0] := #2;
  hex    := tmp;
end;
```

{
  "Yes" returns true or false depending on the input in the
  string, "Answer."
}

```
function Yes : boolean;
var
  i : byte;

begin
  for i := 1 to length(Answer) do Answer[i] := UpCase (Answer[i]);
  if (Answer = 'Y') or (Answer = 'YES')
    then Yes := TRUE
    else Yes := FALSE;
end;
```

{
  "Error" is a procedure that outputs text when the program's
  input is unacceptable.
}

```
procedure Error;
begin
  ClrScr;
```

(continued)

```pascal
    writeln;
    writeln('An error has occurred. Please check your drive.');
    writeln('Make sure that the door is closed and that a ');
    writeln('diskette is in the drive. A read error occurred.');
    Halt;
  end;


{
  "FrameIt" produces a frame around the border of the input
  area at the bottom of the screen.
}

procedure FrameIt;
var  i : integer;

begin
  GotoXY( 1,21); Write(chr(218));  { Upper left corner symbol.  }
  GotoXY(79,21); Write(chr(191));  { Upper right corner symbol. }
  GotoXY( 1,25); Write(chr(192));  { Lower left corner symbol.  }
  GotoXY(79,25); Write(chr(217));  { Lower right corner symbol. }

  for i := 22 to 24 do
    begin
      GotoXY( 1, i);  Write(chr(179)); { Vertical symbol.    }
      GotoXY(79, i);  Write(chr(179));
    end;

  for i := 2 to 78 do
    begin
      GotoXY(i, 21); Write(chr(196));  { Horizontal symbol.  }
      GotoXY(i, 25); Write(chr(196));
    end;
end;


{
  "Initialize" is a procedure that sets all variables to their default
  values.
}

procedure Initialize;
begin
  ClrScr;
  FrameIt;
  Continue := False;
  DriveNumber  := 0;
  TrackNumber  := 1;
  HeadNumber   := 1;
  SectorNumber := 1;
  FillChar( Regs,SizeOf(Regs),0 ); {Init the registers}
  FillChar( SectorBuffer,SizeOf(SectorBuffer),0 ); {Init the buffer}
end;
```

{
"ClearFrame" clears the portion of the screen which is used for input
and places the cursor in the right location for the next time
that a write is made to that area.
}

```
procedure ClearFrame;
var  i,j : integer;

begin
  Window(2,22,78,24);
  ClrScr;
  Window(1,1,80,25);
  GotoXY( 2,22);
end;
```

{
"Display" writes the buffer contents to the screen in hexadecimal
by calling the function, "Hex." Control characters are filtered
out. This insures a clean screen display.
}

```
procedure Display;
var
  i : integer;
  j : integer;
begin
  for i := 0 to 511 do
    begin
      j := i + 26;
      GotoXY((2 * (j mod 26)) + 1, j div 26);        {home := 1,1}
      write (hex(SectorBuffer[i]));
      GotoXY((j mod 26) + 54, j div 26);
      if (SectorBuffer[i] > 31)
        then write(chr(SectorBuffer[i]))
        else write(chr(46));
    end;
  writeln;
end;
```

{
"AskForInput" gets all the necessary input from the user of the program.
Since this is a fairly complicated program that requires many parameters
from the user, this is preferable than trying to force the user to give
all the parameters at the command line.
}

```
procedure AskForInput;
begin
```

(continued)

```pascal
    ClearFrame;
    write('What drive do you want to look at (0 = A:)? ');
    readln(DriveNumber);
    if DriveNumber > 1        { If you want to edit bytes on your hard }
      then                    { disk then take out these lines, but you }
        begin                 { do so at your own risk!                 }
          ClrScr;
          writeln('It is not a good idea to fool around with Hard Drives!!!');
          Halt;
        end;
    ClearFrame;
    write('What track do you want to see? ');
    readln(TrackNumber);
    ClearFrame;
    write('What side (0 or 1)? ');
    readln(HeadNumber);
    ClearFrame;
    write('What sector? ');
    readln(SectorNumber);
    ClearFrame;
    write('Drive ',DriveNumber,', Track ',TrackNumber,', Side ',
          HeadNumber,', and Sector ',SectorNumber,'.');
  end;


{
  "AskForEdit" is used to ask the user if he wants to edit any
  bytes in the sector. If he does, then further input is requested
  and ultimately the changes are written to the buffer, but not the
  disk--not yet at least!
}

procedure AskForEdit;
begin
  if Yes
    then
      begin
        Continue := True;
        ClearFrame;
        write('Which byte (0 through 511)? ');
        readln(By);
        ClearFrame;
        writeln('Byte number ',By,' is now ',SectorBuffer[By],'.');
        GotoXY (2,23);
        write('What do you want to change it to? ');
        readln(NewValue);
        SectorBuffer[By] := NewValue;
        ClearFrame;
        write('Byte number ',By,' is now ',SectorBuffer[By],'.');
      end
    else Continue := False;
end;


{
```

```
"DisplayEdit" displays any changes that were made with the "AskForEdit"
procedure. Checks are made to insure that control characters are not
written to the screen. Characters below character 46 could wreck havoc
on the screen display.
}

procedure DisplayEdit;
var
  i : integer;

begin
  i := By + 26;
  GotoXY((2 * (i mod 26)) + 1, i div 26);       {home := 1,1}
  write (hex(SectorBuffer[By]));
  GotoXY((i mod 26) + 54, i div 26);
  if (SectorBuffer[By] > 31)
    then write(chr(SectorBuffer[By]))
    else write(chr(46));                        {Avoid control characters.}
end;


{
  "ReadDiskAndMakeEdits" is almost a main program loop that calls
  other functions and procedures to get the work done in this
  program. It is a separate procedure just to make the main program
  look tidy.
}

procedure ReadDiskAndMakeEdits;
begin
  if SectorRead (DriveNumber,TrackNumber,HeadNumber,SectorNumber) = 0
    then Display
    else
      begin
        ClearFrame;
        Error;
      end;
  Repeat
    ClearFrame;
    write ('Edit bytes? ');
    readln (Answer);
    AskForEdit;
    if Continue then DisplayEdit;
  Until not Continue;
  ClearFrame;
end;


{
  "WriteBuffer" is another chunk of code that could be in the main
  program loop, but is separated for appearance.
}
```

(continued)

```pascal
procedure WriteBuffer;
begin
  write ('Do you want to write the new sector to disk? ');
  readln (Answer);
  if Yes
    then
      begin
        if SectorWrite (DriveNumber,TrackNumber,HeadNumber,SectorNumber) = 0
          then
            begin
              ClearFrame;
              writeln ('Successful write.')
            end
          else
            begin
              ClearFrame;
              writeln ('Error in write.');
            end;
      end;
end;


begin   {Main Program}
  Initialize;
  AskForInput;
  ReadDiskAndMakeEdits;
  WriteBuffer;
  Delay(1000);
  ClrScr;
end.
```

FINDFILE

Type External

Purpose This utility searches for any file in any subdirectory of a hard disk (or floppy, if you use subdirectories on a floppy) and reports all occurrences. It begins its search at the root directory.

Format FINDFILE
or
FINDFILE filename.exe
or
FINDFILE *.*
or
FINDFILE ??CK.U

The term *filename.ext* is the name of any file that you are looking for.
The symbols *.* are the normal DOS wild-card characters. ?? is another wild-card character that can be used. Any filename extension and wild-card combination that the DIR command permits, this utility will also permit.

FINDFILE is one of those commands that everyone wishes Microsoft had included—especially so when you switch over to a hard disk with the so-called tree-structured subdirectories. It can be a nuisance trying to find a file or even trying to find out if you have different versions of the same program taking up space in two different parts of your hard disk.

Several calls to DOS functions are made to get the information. FINDFILE is not the type of program that can be written in plain old Pascal. This program requires plenty of low-level machine code-like calls to the operating system. For example, a call is made to set up a buffer for the information that DOS returns on the other calls. Then calls are made to find all the subdirectories starting at the current working directory. After this, those subdirectories are scanned for files that match the supplied parameter on the command line. Once a file that matches is found, its location (path) and the filename are printed. Because of the way the program is set up, you can get a complete list of all the files in the disk drive by typing "FINDFILE *.*" at the DOS prompt. It does not matter what directory you are in.

Although FINDFILE is comprehensive, it can be expanded. The program has a record structure called **DirectoryEntry** that is used as the buffer for the Disk Transfer Area (DTA—a buffer that DOS requires for any type of directory searching). This record structure is divided into all the components of a disk directory: the file's name, size, and date, and the time of the last update. Through some more programming, you can decipher these bytes and produce results that are equal to the DOS directory command while retaining the advantage of spanning across subdirectory walls.

Example 1—Getting help on the command
    C> FINDFILE
    help text is printed

Example 2—Getting a listing of all the files on your hard disk
    C> findfile *.*
    long output if you have a large drive with many files on it.

Example 3—Finding all files that end in the extension **.PAS**.
    C> findfile *.
    output of program follows

Example 4—Finding files that match a criterion
    C> findfile ??r.a??
    files like the following would match:
        car.arc
        bar.art
        par.all
        ,...>

Program

```
Program Findfile;
{
    Title       : FILE FINDER      Version 2.00
    Author      : Robert Alonso
    Versions    : 1.00 May 5, 1986
                  2.00 October 23, 1986

    Purpose     : This program can be used to find a file or
                  several files that match what is presented
                  in the DOS command line. Wildcard characters
                  "?" and "*" are allowed.

    I/O Requirements : The program will work on MS-DOS and PC-DOS
                  computers.
}
```

```
type
  RegRec     =
   record
     AX, BX, CX, DX, BP, SI, DI, DS, ES, Flags : Integer;
   end;

  DirectoryEntry  =
   record
     Useless    : array [1..21] of byte;
     Attribute  : byte;
     Time       : integer;
     Date       : integer;
     FileSize   : array [1..2] of integer;
     FileName   : array [1..13] of char;
   end;

  DirectoryArray = array [1..192] of string[255];
  MaxString      = string[255];

var
  Regs         : RegRec;
  DTA          : DirectoryEntry;
  Dirs         : DirectoryArray;
  Name,
  SearchMask,
  Mask         : string[13];
  Drive        : string[2];
  Path,
  OrigPath,
  NewPath      : MaxString;
  ErrorCode,
  Option,
  NumEntries,
  Counter      : byte;
  Found        : boolean;

{
  "UpItsCase" is a function that takes a string of any length and
  sets all of the characters in the string to upper case. Its handy
  for comparing strings.
}

function UpItsCase (SourceStr : MaxString) : MaxString;
var
  I    : integer;

begin
  for I := 1 to length(SourceStr) do
    SourceStr[I] := UpCase(SourceStr[I]);
  UpItsCase := SourceStr
end;
```

(continued)

```
{
  "NoFiles" is a procedure that outputs text when the program
  finds no files on the drive that satisfy the command line
  parameter.
}

procedure NoFiles;
begin
  writeln;
  writeln('No files match the search string. Try letters');
  writeln('in conjunction with wild cards. You may have');
  writeln('mispelled the search string.');
end;


{
  "Help" is a procedure that outputs text that guides the program's
  user. All output is sent to the current output device--usually the
  screen.
}

procedure Help;
begin
  writeln;
  writeln('FINDFILE will scan your entire disk for any search');
  writeln('pattern that you specify at the command line.');
  writeln('Both DOS wildcard characters are allowed. If you');
  writeln('want to list all the files in all the directories');
  writeln('you can simply type, "FINDFILE *.*" and every file');
  writeln('in every subdirectory will be listed.');
  writeln;
  writeln('Example: C>findfile *.com');
  Halt;
end;


{
  "Initialize" is a procedure that sets all variables to their default
  values.
}

procedure Initialize;
begin
  GetDir(0,Path);
  OrigPath := Path;
  Drive := Copy(Path,Pred(Pos(':',Path)),2);
  Path := '\';
  Option := 255;
  ErrorCode := 0;
  FillChar (DTA,SizeOf(DTA),0);
  Mask := '????????.???' + chr(0);
  NumEntries := 0;
  Counter := 0;
  Found := False;
end;
```

```
{
  "ParseCommandLine" is a procedure that checks if any data was input
  at the DOS command line. If no data is there, then the "Help"
  procedure is executed and the program is halted. Otherwise, the
  SearchMask variable is set equal to the text on the command line.
}

procedure ParseCommandLine;
begin
  if ParamCount = 0
    then Help
    else
      begin
        SearchMask := ParamStr (1);
        if length(SearchMask) > 12
          then
            begin
              writeln;
              writeln('Your search parameter is too long!');
              writeln('The maximum is 12 characters.');
              Halt;
            end;
        SearchMask := UpItsCase(SearchMask);
      end;
end;


{
  "SetDTA" tells DOS what area of memory to use as a buffer for its
  transfer of data. The area called DTA is a record that is precisely
  broken up into meaningful entries. Look at the type definitions
  and you will see what I mean.
}

procedure SetDTA;
begin
  Regs.AX := $1A00;
  Regs.DS := Seg(DTA);
  Regs.DX := Ofs(DTA);
  MSDos (Regs);
end;


{
  "FindFirst" does exactly what its name implies. It uses a DOS function
  to find the first file that matches the mask.
}

procedure FindFirst;
begin
  Regs.AX := $4E00;
  Regs.DS := Seg(Mask);
  Regs.DX := Ofs(Mask) + 1;
```

(continued)

```
  Regs.CX := Option;
  MSDos (Regs);
  ErrorCode := lo(Regs.AX);
end;


{
  "FindNext" uses another DOS function to find the next matching file.
  As with "FindFirst," an error is indicated by a non-zero value in the
  low byte of register AX.
}

procedure FindNext;
begin
  Regs.AX := $4F00;
  Regs.CX := Option;
  MSDos (Regs);
  ErrorCode := lo(Regs.AX);
end;


{
  "ParseDTA" removes the name and extension from the DTA to a string.
  This makes it easier to manipulate and print.
}

procedure ParseDTA;
var
  i : byte;

begin
  i := 1;
  repeat
    Name[i] := DTA.FileName[i];
    i := i + 1
  until DTA.FileName[i] = #0;
  Name[0] := chr(i - 1);
end;


{
  "DisplayEntry" calls the "ParseDTA" procedure and prints out the
  name that the procedure gives it. If there are no files on the
  disk that match the search string, this routine should never
  be executed. Because of this, the variable Found is set to equal
  True if this routine is executed.
}

procedure DisplayEntry;
begin
  ParseDTA;
  writeln(Name);
  Found := True;
end;
```

```
{
 "GetEntries" will get all files that match the search
 string and print out the path in which the file is found.
}

procedure GetEntries(CurPath : MaxString);
begin
  ChDir(CurPath);
  FindFirst;
  if ErrorCode = 0
    then
      begin
        writeln;
        writeln('Path: ',Drive+CurPath);
        writeln;
      end;
  while ErrorCode = 0 do
    begin
      DisplayEntry;
      FindNext;
    end;
end;


{
 "DoSubs" makes sure that the "GetEntries" routine searches through
 all known directories. These are in an array that "GetDirectories"
 sets up.
}

procedure DoSubs;
begin
  while Counter <> NumEntries do
    begin
      Counter := Counter + 1;
      NewPath := Dirs[Counter];
      GetEntries(NewPath);
    end;
end;


{
 "ScanForDirectories" goes through the entire disk trying to find
 directories. This is necessary, because other routines depend on
 this information to insure that everything has been checked. You
 will notice that the coding for this procedure is very similar to
 the coding for the procedure "GetEntries."
}

procedure ScanForDirectories(CurPath : MaxString);
begin
  ChDir(CurPath);
  FindFirst;
```

(continued)

```pascal
  repeat
    ParseDTA;
    if ((DTA.Attribute and 16) = 16) and (Name <> '.') and (Name <> '..')
      then
        begin
          NumEntries := NumEntries + 1;
          if CurPath = '\'
            then CurPath := '';
          Dirs[NumEntries] := CurPath + '\' + Name;
        end;
    FindNext;
  until ErrorCode <> 0;
end;


{
  "DoDirSubs" sets up the array of subdirectories for the calling
  procedure "GetDirectories." This procedure is similar to the
  "DoSubs" procedure above.
}

procedure DoDirSubs;
begin
  while Counter <> NumEntries do
    begin
      Counter := Counter + 1;
      NewPath := Dirs[Counter];
      ScanForDirectories(NewPath);
    end;
end;

{
  "GetDirectories" calls other routines to get the names of all
  subdirectories (including hidden ones) into an array that is
  later used by the program. This routine is also used as a way
  to reset the values of variables that are used more than once.
}

procedure GetDirectories;
var
  i : byte;

begin
  ScanForDirectories(Path);
  DoDirSubs;
  ChDir(Path);                   { This is like a second Initialize }
  Counter := 0;                  { procedure. All used variables    }
  ErrorCode := 0;                { need to be reset.                }
  Option := Option and 239;
  for i := 1 to length(SearchMask) do
    begin
      Mask[i] := SearchMask[i];
    end;
  Mask[i + 1] := chr(0);
end;
```

```
begin  {Main Program}
  Initialize;
  ParseCommandLine;
  SetDTA;
  GetDirectories;
  GetEntries(Path);
  DoSubs;
  ChDir(OrigPath);
  if not Found
    then NoFiles;
end.
```

MOVE

Type External

Purpose This utility simplifies hard disk maintenance. Moving a file from one directory to another is made much faster.

Format MOVE
or
MOVE c:\ sub1 \ filename.ext c:\ sub2 \ filename.ext

The *c:* is the drive where the file resides. It can be any drive, not just a hard disk drive.
sub1 is the subdirectory where the file currently resides, and *sub2* is the subdirectory where you want to move the file.
The term *filename.ext* is the name of the file and its extension.

This command accomplishes what normally takes two commands in less time than it takes to just execute one of them. Normally, when you want to move a file from one subdirectory to another, you have to copy the file from the original subdirectory to the target subdirectory and then delete the original file. Besides being a two-step process that is time-consuming, it can also be impossible to do at times. If you have subdirectories on a floppy diskette, you may not have enough space on the disk to accommodate two copies of the same file—the original and the copy in the target subdirectory. It is here where having a MOVE command can really save you time. MOVE never actually moves your file; instead it moves the directory entry of the file—which is why it takes much less time than a copy and delete or even just one of those operations. MOVE works where a copy and delete fails because you don't need space for two copies of the file—just enough space for the directory entry which is seldom a problem.

MOVE is most useful, however, on a hard disk system. MOVE can be a real timesaver when you need to rearrange several files from one subdirectory to another.

If you try to move a file from one drive to another you will not get any results. Trying to so move a file is impossible because, as previously stated, the file isn't really moved.

Programmer's Info

MOVE works because DOS has a rename function. This rename function can be used for both renaming the filename and moving its subdirectory entry. If you wish to look up the function in the DOS Technical Reference Manual, it is function 56H.

Turbo Pascal's rename function uses DOS' function and can thus also move subdirectories. The procedure MOVEIT in the program does all the work. You could rewrite the program without the help text and error messages and still get the same results.

Example 1—Getting help on the command
C>move
help text is printed

Example 2—Moving a file called SECRET.DOC from subdirectory WS to subdirectory SECRET
C>move c:\ ws \ secret.doc c:\ secret \ secret.doc

Example 3—Moving a file called SECRET.DOC from subdirectory WS to subdirectory SECRET and calling it MYSECRET.DOC in the destination subdirectory
C>move c:\ ws \ secret.doc c:\ secret \ mysecret.doc

Example 4—Using MOVE to rename a file
C>move secret.doc mysecret.doc

Program

```
Program Move;
{
    Title       : MOVE FILE UTILITY      Version 1.00
    Author      : Robert Alonso
    Versions    : 1.00 December 28, 1985

    Purpose     : This program is used for moving files
                  from one subdirectory to another subdirectory
                  or to the root. It replaces having to copy
                  and delete a file and is much faster.

    I/O Requirements : The program will work on MS-DOS and PC-DOS
                       computers with or without hard disk drives.
}
type
  Name = string[80];

var
  FileInCurrentLocation : Name;
  FileInFutureLocation  : Name;
```

(continued)

{
"Exist" is a function that checks if a file exist in the designated
drive and directory. It returns true or false.
}

```pascal
function Exist (FileName : Name) : boolean;
var
   Fil       : file;
begin
  assign (Fil, FileName);
  {$I-} reset (Fil) {$I+};
  Exist := (IOresult = 0);
end;
```

{
"Error" is a procedure that outputs text when the program's
input is unacceptable. This procedure will be invoked when the
file that is specified in the command line parameter does not
exist. It will also be invoked if two different drives are
specified. "Move" will only work if the current location and
future location of the file are on the same drive.
}

```pascal
procedure Error;
begin
  writeln;
  writeln('File does not exist!');
  writeln;
  writeln('An error has occurred. Make sure that you have');
  writeln('typed in the name and path of the file correctly');
  writeln('and that the current and future location of the');
  writeln('file are on the same disk drive.');
end;
```

{
"Help" is a procedure that outputs text that guides the program's
user. All output is sent to the current output device--usually the
screen.
}

```pascal
procedure Help;
begin
  writeln;
  writeln('MOVE will quickly move files from one subdirectory');
  writeln('to another or to the root directory of a drive. It');
  writeln('is faster than copying files between subdirectories');
  writeln('because only the directory entry is moved--the file');
  writeln('stays in its original location. Because of this, MOVE');
  writeln('will not move files from drive to drive.');
  writeln;
  writeln('Example: A>move c:\word\text.doc c:\spell\text.doc"');
```

```
  writeln;
  writeln('The example moves the file called, "text.doc" from');
  writeln('subdirectory "word" to subdirectory "spell." Note');
  writeln('that both directories are on drive "c." Once you move');
  writeln('a file, it will only show up in the new directory.');
  Halt;
end;

{
  "ParseCommandLine" is a procedure that checks if any data was input
  at the DOS command line. If no data is there, then the "Help"
  procedure is executed and the program is halted. Otherwise, the
  FileInCurrentLocation variable is set equal to the first text on
  the command line and the variable FileInFutureLocation is set equal
  to the second chunk of text on the command line.
}

procedure ParseCommandLine;
begin
  if ParamCount = 0
    then Help
    else
      begin
        FileInCurrentLocation := ParamStr (1);
        FileInFutureLocation  := ParamStr (2);
      end;
end;

{
  "Move" does the real work in this program. It uses Turbo Pascal's
  "rename" procedure to move the directory entry from the current location
  to the future location specified. If you are interested in some more
  detail on why this works you can study DOS function 56H in a technical
  manual.
}

procedure MoveIt;
var
  Fil       : file;

begin
  assign(Fil, FileInCurrentLocation);
  rename(Fil, FileInFutureLocation);
end;


begin      {Main Program}
  ParseCommandLine;
  if Exist(FileInCurrentLocation)
    then MoveIt
    else Error;
end.
```

CHAPTER 5

Peripheral Utilities

LASER

Type	External
Purpose	This utility is used for setting a Hewlett Packard parallel laser printer to special modes. Special characters like a carriage return and form feed can also be sent.
Format	LASER *or* LASER selector The *selector* can be one of the following: boldon, boldoff, ital, upright, con, coff, lf, ff, cr, esc, reset.

LASER, like PMODE (which follows in this book), is designed to complement the DOS command MODE by adding the features that it is missing. LASER allows you to set various useful modes in a standard parallel Hewlett Packard laser printer. (Modifying it for a serial laser printer should not be very difficult.)

LASER allows you to easily set the printer to bold pitch, italic printing, upright printing, and condensed printing. Combinations of the different modes are also possible, and sending control characters, such as a line feed or, form feed or even a carriage return or escape character, is extremely easy. Resetting the printer, a frequent necessity with the laser printer, is also easy to do with LASER.

If you compare this utility and the one that follows (PMODE), you will notice that there are many similarities in the coding. The reason for this is that LASER was based on PMODE. LASER, like PMODE, is a utility for setting the mode of a printer. LASER, however, is specialized. It works only with the HP LaserJet printer. By comparing LASER and PMODE, you will see how easy it is to modify either one to work with whatever printer you own.

Example 1—Getting help on the command

    A>laser
    help text is printed

Example 2—Setting bold printing on
    A> laser boldon

Example 3—Setting italic printing
    A> laser ital

Example 4—Turning condensed mode off
    A> laser coff

Example 5—Sending a line feed to the printer
    A> laser lf

Example 6—Resetting the printer
    A> laser reset

Program

```
Program Laser;
{
     Title         : SET LASER PRINTER MODE  Version 1.00
     Author        : Robert Alonso
     Versions      : 1.00 January 14, 1986

     Purpose       : Program that sets the HP Laserjet Printer
                     to several different modes. The available
                     modes are normal, bold on, bold off, italic
                     on, italic off, compressed on, and compressed
                     off. Special control codes such as line feed,
                     form feed, carriage return, escape and reset
                     can also be sent to the printer.

          I/O Requirements : The program will work on MS-DOS and PC-DOS
                             computers that are equipped with the HP
                             Laserjet Printer.
}

const
  LineFeed        = #10;
  FormFeed        = #12;
  CarriageReturn  = #13;
  Escape          = #27; { Escape is used with the following modes: }
  Reset_Char      = 'E';
  CompressedOn    = '(s16.6H';  { 16.66 CPI (characters per inch) }
  CompressedOff   = '(s10H';    { 10 CPI                          }
  ItalicOn        = '(s1S';
  Up_right        = '(s0S';
  Bold_On         = '(s3B';
  Bold_Off        = '(s0B';
```

(continued)

```pascal
type
  ModeType = (lf,ff,cr,esc,boldon,boldoff,ital,upright,
              con,coff,reset,NotValid);
  MaxString = string[255];

var
  Code    : ModeType;
  Mode    : string[8];
  ModeIn  : array [ModeType] of string[8];
  Found   : boolean;
```

{
  "UpItsCase" is a function that takes a string of any length and
  sets all of the characters in the string to upper case. Its handy
  for comparing strings.
}

```pascal
function UpItsCase (SourceStr : MaxString) : MaxString;
var
  I       : integer;
begin
  for I := 1 to length(SourceStr) do
    SourceStr[I] := UpCase(SourceStr[I]);
  UpItsCase := SourceStr
end;
```

{
  "Error" is a procedure that prints out an error message. This
  procedure is called when the input at the command line does not
  match any of the legal choices or when it matches, "NotValid."
}

```pascal
procedure Error;
begin
  writeln;
  writeln('An error has ocurred. You have either typed');
  writeln('a mode that is unacceptable or have included');
  writeln('characters that are not necessary.');
  writeln;
  writeln('Example: A>LASER lf');
  Halt;
end;
```

{
  "Help" is a procedure that outputs text that guides the program's
  user. All output is sent to the current output device--usually the
  screen.
}

```
procedure Help;
begin
  writeln;
  writeln('LASER helps you set your printer"s mode and also makes');
  writeln('it easy for you to send some control characters to it.');
  writeln('It is specifically designed to work with the HP Laser');
  writeln('Printer. Example: LASER mode');
  writeln;
  writeln('Available modes:');
  writeln;
  writeln('boldon = Bold On        boldoff = Bold Off');
  writeln('ital    = Italic On     upright = Italic Off');
  writeln('con     = Compressed On    coff    = Compressed Off');
  writeln('lf      = Line Feed        ff      = Form Feed');
  writeln('cr      = Carriage Return  esc     = Escape');
  writeln('reset = Resets The Printer');
  writeln;
  writeln('Developed by, Robert Alonso. All rights reserved.');
  Halt;
end;


{
  "Initialize" does exactly what the name implies. It is used in this
  utility to intialize an array that is used in converting strings to
  the defined scalar type, "ModeType."
}

procedure Initialize;
begin
  ModeIn[lf]       := 'LF';
  ModeIn[ff]       := 'FF';
  ModeIn[cr]       := 'CR';
  ModeIn[esc]      := 'ESC';
  ModeIn[boldon]   := 'BOLDON';
  ModeIn[boldoff]  := 'BOLDOFF';
  ModeIn[ital]     := 'ITAL';
  ModeIn[upright]  := 'UPRIGHT';
  ModeIn[con]      := 'CON';
  ModeIn[coff]     := 'COFF';
  ModeIn[reset]    := 'RESET';
  ModeIn[NotValid] := 'NOTVALID';
end;


{
  "ParseCommandLine" is a procedure that checks if any data was input
  at the DOS command line. If no data is there, then the "Help"
  procedure is executed and the program is halted. Otherwise, the
  Mode string variable is set equal to the text on the command line.
}
```

(continued)

```pascal
procedure ParseCommandLine;
begin
 if ParamCount = 0
   then Help
   else
     begin
       Mode := ParamStr (1);
       Mode := UpItsCase(Mode);
     end;
end;
```

{
 "Convert_To_Scalar" is the routine that does the actual
 conversion of a string to a defined scalar type, "ModeType."
}

```pascal
procedure Convert_To_Scalar;
begin
 Found := False;
 Code := If;
 repeat
   if ModeIn[Code] = Mode
     then Found := True
     else Code := Succ(Code);
 until Found or (Code = NotValid);
 if not Found
   then Error;
end;
```

{
 "PrintControlCodes" sends output to the printer based on the
 conversion that takes place in the "Convert_To_Scalar" procedure.
 This section may have to be modified if your printer uses radically
 different control codes for setting these modes. Ideally, you
 should be able to modify this utility by just making a few changes
 in the constant declaration section at the beginning.
}

```
procedure PrintControlCodes;
begin
  case Code of
    lf      : write(lst,LineFeed);
    ff      : write(lst,FormFeed);
    cr      : write(lst,CarriageReturn);
    esc     : write(lst,Escape);
    con     : write(lst,Escape,CompressedOn);
    coff    : write(lst,Escape,CompressedOff);
    ital    : write(lst,Escape,ItalicOn);
    upright : write(lst,Escape,Up_right);
    boldon  : write(lst,Escape,Bold_On);
    boldoff : write(lst,Escape,Bold_Off);
    reset   : write(lst,Escape,Reset_Char);
    NotValid : Error;
  end;
end;


begin     {Main Program}
  Initialize;
  ParseCommandLine;
  Convert_To_Scalar;
  PrintControlCodes;
end.
```

PMODE

Type   External

Purpose   This utility is used for setting the printer's mode. Enlarged, condensed, emphasized, and other modes can be easily set. Special characters like a carriage return and form feed can also be sent.

Format   PMODE
or
PMODE selector

The *selector* can be one of the following: dwon, dwoff, con, coff, eon, eoff, dson, dsoff, lf, ff, cr.

Microsoft included a command called MODE that is extremely versatile. With it you can set the line width and spacing of the printer, configure various communication parameters, and redirect printer output to a serial port. Additionally, an obscure use of MODE allows you to center the image on a non-IBM display attached to the color/graphics adapter. But perhaps the most common use of MODE is to select the active display: monochrome, color, or black and white. PMODE is designed to complement MODE by adding the features that it is missing. PMODE allows you to set various useful modes in a standard IBM- or Epson-compatible printer.

PMODE will work with numerous printers because many of the printers available on the market are Epson compatible. It allows you to easily set the printer to double width printing, condensed printing, emphasized printing, and double strike printing. Combinations of the different modes are also possible, and sending control characters, such as a line feed or a form feed or even a carriage return, is extremely easy.

The following is a list of a few of the printers that PMODE works on:

All Epson printers

IBM Proprinter

IBM Graphics Printer

Texas Instruments 99/4 Impact Printer

NEC P5 and NEC P7

Genicom 3014 (Epson-configured)

Okidata ML IBM

Okidata ML with Plug 'N Play

Okidata PaceMark 2410 (IBM-configured)

Wang PM-0016

Example 1—Getting help on the command
```
A>pmode
help text is printed
```

Example 2—Setting double width on
```
A>pmode dwon
```

Example 3—Setting condensed on
```
A>pmode con
```

Example 4—Turning condensed mode off
```
A>pmode coff
```

Example 5—Sending a line feed to the printer
```
A>pmode lf
```

Example 6—Sending a carriage return to the printer
```
A>pmode cr
```

Program

```
Program Pmode;
{
    Title      : SET PRINTER MODE      Version 2.00
    Author     : Robert Alonso
    Versions   : 1.00 October 5, 1985
                 2.00 November 5, 1985

    Purpose    : Program that sets the IBM Graphics Printer
                 to several different modes. The available
                 modes are normal, double width, compressed,
                 emphasized and double printing. Additionally,
                 it facilitates the sending of several control
                 codes to the printer (ie., line feed, form
                 feed and carriage return).

    I/O Requirements : The program will work on MS-DOS and PC-DOS
                       computers that are equipped with the IBM
                       Graphics Printer.
}
```

(continued)

```pascal
const
  LineFeed       = #10;
  FormFeed       = #12; { These values are standard for IBM, but }
  CarriageReturn = #13; { if you own a non-compatible printer you }
  DoubleWidthOn  = #14; { can substitute that printer's values for }
  CompressedOn   = #15; { these. Your printer's manual will help. }
  CompressedOff  = #18;
  DoubleWidthOff = #20;
  Escape         = #27; { Escape is used with the following modes: }
  EmphasizedOn   = #69; {27,69}
  EmphasizedOff  = #70; {27,70}
  DoubleStrikeOn = #71; {27,71}
  DoubleStrikeOff = #72; {27,72}

type
  ModeType  = (lf,ff,cr,dwon,dwoff,con,coff,eon,eoff,dson,dsoff,NotValid);
  MaxString = string[255];

var
  Code    : ModeType;
  Mode    : string[8];
  ModeIn  : array [ModeType] of string[8];
  Found   : boolean;


{
  "UpItsCase" is a function that takes a string of any length and
  sets all of the characters in the string to upper case. Its handy
  for comparing strings.
}

function UpItsCase (SourceStr : MaxString) : MaxString;
var
  I       : integer;
begin
  for I := 1 to length(SourceStr) do
    SourceStr[I] := UpCase(SourceStr[I]);
  UpItsCase := SourceStr
end;


{
  "Error" is a procedure that prints out an error message. This
  procedure is called when the input at the command line does not
  match any of the legal choices or when it matches, "NotValid."
}


procedure Error;
begin
  writeln;
  writeln('An error has ocurred. You have either typed');
  writeln('a mode that is unacceptable or have included');
  writeln('characters that are not necessary.');
```

```
      writeln;
      writeln('Example: A>PMODE lf');
      Halt;
  end;


  {
    "Help" is a procedure that outputs text that guides the program's
    user. All output is sent to the current output device--usually the
    screen.
  }

  procedure Help;
  begin
    writeln;
    writeln('PMODE helps you set your printer''s mode and also makes');
    writeln('it easy for you to send some control characters to it.');
    writeln('It is specifically designed to work with the IBM Graphics');
    writeln('Printer. Example: PMODE mode');
    writeln;
    writeln('Available modes:');
    writeln;
    writeln('dwon   = Double Width On      dwoff = Double Width Off');
    writeln('con    = Condensed On         coff  = Condensed Off');
    writeln('eon    = Emphasized On        eoff  = Emphasized Off');
    writeln('dson   = Double Strike On     dsoff = Double Strike Off');
    writeln('lf     = Line Feed         ff       = Form Feed');
    writeln('cr     = Carriage Return');
    Halt;
  end;


  {
    "Initialize" does exactly what the name implies. It is used in this
    utility to intialize an array that is used in converting strings to
    the defined scalar type, "ModeType."
  }

  procedure Initialize;
  begin
    ModeIn[lf]       := 'LF';
    ModeIn[ff]       := 'FF';
    ModeIn[cr]       := 'CR';
    ModeIn[dwon]     := 'DWON';
    ModeIn[dwoff]    := 'DWOFF';
    ModeIn[con]      := 'CON';
    ModeIn[coff]     := 'COFF';
    ModeIn[eon]      := 'EON';
    ModeIn[eoff]     := 'EOFF';
    ModeIn[dson]     := 'DSON';
    ModeIn[dsoff]    := 'DSOFF';
    ModeIn[NotValid] := 'NOTVALID';
  end;
```

(continued)

{
"ParseCommandLine" is a procedure that checks if any data was input
at the DOS command line. If no data is there, then the "Help"
procedure is executed and the program is halted. Otherwise, the
Mode string variable is set equal to the text on the command line.
}

```
procedure ParseCommandLine;
begin
  if ParamCount = 0
    then Help
    else
      begin
        Mode := ParamStr (1);
        Mode := UpItsCase(Mode);
      end;
end;
```

{
"Convert_To_Scalar" is the routine that does the actual
conversion of a string to a defined scalar type, "ModeType."
}

```
procedure Convert_To_Scalar;
begin
  Found := False;
  Code := lf;
  repeat
    if ModeIn[Code] = Mode
      then Found := True
      else Code := Succ(Code);
  until Found or (Code = NotValid);
  if not Found
    then Error;
end;
```

{
"PrintControlCodes" sends output to the printer based on the
conversion that takes place in the "Convert_To_Scalar" procedure.
This section may have to be modified if your printer uses radically
different control codes for setting these modes. Ideally, you
should be able to modify this utility by just making a few changes
in the constant declaration section at the beginning.
}

```
procedure PrintControlCodes;
begin
  case Code of
    lf    : write(lst,LineFeed);
    ff    : write(lst,FormFeed);
    cr    : write(lst,CarriageReturn);
```

```
      dwon     : write(lst,DoubleWidthOn);
      dwoff    : write(lst,DoubleWidthOff);
      con      : write(lst,CompressedOn);
      coff     : write(lst,CompressedOff);
      eon      : write(lst,Escape,EmphasizedOn);
      eoff     : write(lst,Escape,EmphasizedOff);
      dson     : write(lst,Escape,DoubleStrikeOn);
      dsoff    : write(lst,Escape,DoubleStrikeOff);
      NotValid : Error;
    end;
  end;


begin     {Main Program}
  Initialize;
  ParseCommandLine;
  Convert_To_Scalar;
  PrintControlCodes;
end.
```

CHAPTER 6

Procedures and Functions— Programming Notes

All the utilities in this book rely on certain key procedures and functions that do most of the work. And almost all the utilities share some procedures that are common to all. For example, the **Help** and **Error** procedures are found in almost all the programs in the book. They contain different text messages within each utility but, nonetheless have the same function and are more similar than different. **ParseCommandLine** is another one of these universal procedures. If you figure out how the following procedures work and why they are included in the different programs in the book, you are well on your way toward writing your own Turbo Pascal utilities.

The procedures and functions that are explained in this chapter are in alphabetical order. So if you are working on one of the utilities in the book and run across a routine that you want to have further explained, it is very easy to look it up in this chapter. This chapter can essentially become your quick reference guide.

BEEPTONE

BeepTone is one of the easiest procedures in this book to understand. It simply sends an ASCII character 7 to the screen to produce a bell sound. ASCII, which stands for the American Standard Code for Information Interchange, defines 96 displayable characters and 32 control characters. In this standard, character 7 is defined as the bell sound and can thus be used with little fear for compatibility on differing computer systems. It will always generate the bell sound. Since the ASCII was adopted in the early 1960s, most computers—even a majority of mainframes—use the standard. In the procedure, the terms *bell* and *time* have been previously defined.

```
procedure BeepTone;
begin
  write (bell);
  delay (time);
end;
```

CALLCHMOD

Microsoft DOS and PC-DOS have a set of functions that can be called by programs. These functions are all executed by setting the AH register of the microprocessor to the function number and calling an interrupt 21. Turbo Pascal, unlike other high-level languages, facilitates calling these functions by providing a command called **MsDos**. By setting up the parameters for a function call and then using this Turbo Pascal facility, you can write truly powerful utilities. In fact, many of the utilities in this book would not work at all if Turbo did not provide this facility.

CallChmod uses a rarely mentioned function that allows the modifying of a file's attribute byte. The function number is 67. As you can see, some heavy-duty preparation is needed to use this function. A buffer must be set up with the name and path of the file that you want to alter. Some checking is done before changing a file's attribute to ensure that subdirectories are not damaged. By changing the value in the AL register, you can use this procedure to read the attribute byte and also to change it.

```
procedure CallChmod;
var i : integer;
begin
  DirectoryEntry := UpltsCase(DirectoryEntry) + chr(0);
  Regs.DS := Seg(DirectoryEntry);
  Regs.DX := Ofs(DirectoryEntry) + 1;
  Regs.AH := 67;   { AH is set to 67 for the function call.   }
  Regs.AL := 0;    { if AL := 0 then attribute is returned in CL. }
  MsDos(Regs);     { Get the current attribute.                }
  CurrentAttrib := Regs.CL;

  if (CurrentAttrib = 0) or (CurrentAttrib = 2) or (CurrentAttrib = 3)
    then Error;
```

(continued)

```
if (CurrentAttrib and 16 = 16) and (Value = 1)
  then SubMessage;

if (CurrentAttrib = 22) and (Value = 248)
  then Value := CurrentAttrib and 232
  else if (CurrentAttrib = 16) and (Value = 6)
       then Value := 6
       else if Value = 248
            then Value := CurrentAttrib and Value
            else Value := CurrentAttrib or Value;

Regs.DS  := Seg(DirectoryEntry);
Regs.DX  := Ofs(DirectoryEntry) + 1;
Regs.CX  := Value;
Regs.AH  := 67;  { AH is set to 67 for the function call.  }
Regs.AL  := 1;   { if AL := 1 then attribute in CL is set. }
MsDos(Regs);     { Change the attribute.                   }
end;
```

CHECKMEMORYSIZE

The **CheckMemorySize** procedure calls interrupt 18 to return the memory size of the computer in K units. For the most part this interrupt returns only the amount of memory that the system switches are set for. This means that none of the expanded memory boards will be taken into account by this procedure. Interrupt 18 is a ROM-BIOS service and as such is limited. It reports the same information that is stored in segment 0, offset 413 of low memory.

```
procedure CheckMemorySize;
var
  temp : integer;

begin
  intr(18,Regs);
  temp := Regs.AX;
  writeln('Memory            : ',temp,'K');
end;
```

CLOSEFILES

The **CloseFiles** procedure is pretty standard in all the utilities that open files for input or output. In all programming languages, when a file is opened, it must be closed to make sure that it is properly stored and that all DOS buffers are sent to the disk.

```
procedure CloseFiles;
begin
  close (WorkNameIn);
  close (WorkNameOut);
end;
```

CONVERTTOSCALAR

The **ConvertToScalar** function converts a string that is input at the command line into a scalar type that can be used in the program as part of a case statement. Many neophyte Pascal programmers don't realize that if a string is input it can't be used in a case statement to execute other functions or even generate output. An array of all the possible strings that are acceptable input must be set up prior to calling this routine. Once that array is set up, this function scans it and compares the string that was given as input to the ones in the array. While it scans, it also increments a counter called Choice. Once the procedure is finished, it either returns a value or exits to the **Error** procedure.

```
function ConvertToScalar(Mode : InString) : byte;
begin
  Found := False;
  Code  := Black;
  Choice := 0;
  repeat
    if ColorIn[Code] = Mode
      then Found := True
      else
        begin
          Code := Succ(Code);
          Choice := Choice + 1;
        end;
  until Found or (Code = NotValid);
  if not Found
    then Error
    else ConvertToScalar := Choice;
end;
```

COPYRIGHT

The procedure **Copyright** scans the entire BIOS and Fixed Disk ROM area for the three letters "Cop" that are found in the word "Copyright" or "Copr." This is done to find out the maker of the ROM chips, typically the manufacturer of the PC. This won't be the case on some of the inexpensive clones that have illegal or questionable ROM chips.

You will find this procedure valuable when evaluating machines that are from unknown origins. It uses an absolute array located on the ROM chip itself to scan the area quickly. Considering that it must scan the entire ROM area, if a copyright message is not found, this routine is extremely fast and compact.

The nested "if then" statements are used to make the comparison faster. If the first character is not found, then a check for the next is not made, and if just the first is found then the third check is not made. Writing the procedure this way saves a considerable amount of time.

```
procedure Copyright (WhichROM : string4);
type
  ROMchip  = array [1..8092] of byte;

var
  BIOS    : ROMchip absolute $FE00:$0000;
  FD      : ROMchip absolute $C800:$0000;
  ROM     : ROMchip;
  i,
  j       : integer;
  temp1,
  temp2,
  temp3   : byte;

begin
  writeln;
  i := 0;
  j := 0;
  if WhichROM = 'BIOS'
    then
      begin
        ROM := BIOS;
        write('ROM BIOS Identification : ');
      end
    else
      begin
        ROM := FD;
        write('Fixed Disk ROM Id    : ');
      end;
```

```
if ((ROM[i+1] = $55) and (ROM[i+2] = $AA)) or (WhichROM = 'BIOS')
  then
    begin
      repeat        {Search for 'Cop'}
        i := i + 1;
        temp1 := ROM[i];
        temp2 := ROM[i + 1];
        temp3 := ROM[i + 2];
        if (temp1 = ord('C')) or (temp1 = ord('c'))
          then            { Done this way to speed up search. }
            begin
              if (temp2 = ord('O')) or (temp2 = ord('o'))
                then          { If first condition is not met,   }
                  begin
                    if (temp3 = ord('P')) or (temp3 = ord('p'))
                      then    { others are not tested.           }
                        begin

                          repeat   { Skip string, "Copyright"        }
                            i := i + 1;
                          until ROM[i] = 32;

                          repeat   { Skip spaces, find first character. }
                            i := i + 1;
                          until ROM[i] <> 32;

                          j := i;
                          while ROM[j] in Print do  { Print out meaningful }
                            begin                   { charaters.           }
                              write(chr(ROM[j]));
                              j := j + 1;
                            end;

                          if ROM[j] = 46
                            then write('.');
                        end;
                  end;
            end;
      until (i = 8089) or (j <> 0);
      if j = 0
        then write('Nothing meaningful found');
    end
  else write('ROM not present');
end;
```

DOIO

The **DoIO** procedure is used for getting lines from the input file and sending them out to the list device—usually the printer. A count of how many lines have been output is kept by the program so that a tidy output results. Both a top margin and bottom margin are taken into account.

The procedure continues its work until it encounters the End-Of-File (EOF) marker in the input file.

```
procedure DoIO;
begin
  i := 4;
  for c := 1 to 2 do
    writeln(lst);      { Begin three lines from Top Of Form (TOF) }

  while not eof (WorkNameIn) do
    begin

      if i = 63
        then
          begin                 { Keep three line top and bottom margin. }
            i := 3;             { I'm, of course, assuming a 66 line per }
            for c := 1 to 6 do  { page printer.                          }
              writeln(lst);
          end;

      readln(WorkNameIn, line);
      writeln(lst, line);       { Printer is used as an output text file. }
      i := i + 1;

    end; {While}
end;
```

DOSVERSION

A call to a DOS function is made in the **DOSversion** procedure. The only setup that is required is that the function number, 48, must be placed in the AH register. Upon return from the DOS function, the variable temp is set equal to the version number of DOS, and the result is sent to the current output device—usually the screen.

```
procedure DOSversion;
var
  temp : real;

begin
  Regs.AH := 48;
  MsDos(Regs);
  temp := Regs.AL + (Regs.AH/100);
  writeln('DOS Version         : ',temp:4:2);
end;
```

EMSCHECK

EmsCheck detects the presence of Lotus/Intel/Microsoft (LIM) expanded memory. Expanded memory is a technique devised by the three companies to allow software access to more memory than DOS currently allows. This particular routine gets the address that interrupt $67 points to and then scans that area for the sequence of characters **EMMXXXX0**, which is present if LIM memory is being used. Using a call to one of the interrupts that the LIM specification supports yields the number of pages that are available. Each of these pages represents about 16K of memory. In the routine you will see that there is a line where a multiplication by 16 takes place. That particular line is used to determine the amount of memory that is present in the expanded memory board. The routine is called, **EmsCheck** because the Lotus/Intel/Microsoft specification has also become well known as the expanded memory specification or EMS.

```
procedure EmsCheck;
var
  i,
  Segment,
  Offset  : integer;
  letter  : char;
  name    : string[8];
  manager : file;

begin
  write('Expanded Memory     : ');
  Regs.AH := $35;
  Regs.AL := $67;
  MsDos(Regs);
```

(continued)

```
        Segment := Regs.ES;
        Offset := 9;
        for i := 0 to 8
          do
            begin
              letter := chr(mem[Segment:Offset+i]);
              name[i] := letter;
            end;
        name[0] := #8;
        if name = 'EMMXXXX0'
          then
            begin
              Regs.AH := $42;        { EMM Function 3: Get number of pages. }
              Intr($67,Regs);
              i := Regs.DX * 16;     { number of pages times 16K.            }
              writeln(i,'K');
            end
          else writeln('Not present');
      end;
```

ENCODECHARACTERS

EncodeCharacters is the meat of the program called **Encode**. It reads in a 16K chunk of a file at a time, scrambles it, and then writes it out. The **BlockRead** and **BlockWrite** functions are used because they provide the fastest way to input large amounts of data into a Turbo program.

A counter is maintained that holds the length of the password. This counter is repeatedly decremented to zero as the encoding takes place and is then reset to the length of the password. This ensures that all the bytes in the input file are scrambled with the password in a backwards order. Many small precautions like this are taken in the **Encode** program to make sure that the encrypted output is safe.

The technique that is used is not a particularly exciting algorithm but is instead a practical method for scrambling the bits of each character read from the input file. Using the exclusive-or technique (XOR) ensures that decoding the file will be a straightforward and quick process—provided, of course, that the correct password is entered.

```
        procedure EncodeCharacters;
        var
          i,j,k,
          Ch     : byte;
          CodeCh : char;
```

```
begin
  i := length (Code);
  repeat
    BlockRead(OldFile,Buffer,BufferSize,RecsRead);
    for j := 1 to RecordSize do
      begin
        for k := 1 to BufferSize do
          begin
            CodeCh := Code[i];
            Buffer[j,k] := Buffer[j,k] xor ord(CodeCh);
            i := i - 1;
            if i = 0
              then i := length (Code);
          end;
      end;
    BlockWrite(NewFile,Buffer,RecsRead);
  until RecsRead = 0;
end;
```

ERROR

Error is just a series of writes to the output device that tell the user of a utility that an error of some sort has occurred. Since **Error** is used in a variety of circumstances in the different programs, it was not separated as an include library file (something that Turbo allows you to do and does very well). In general, though, this procedure is invoked when the user's input is at fault.

Notice the use of **Halt** to terminate the program. Some Pascal purists would argue that it is a poor way to terminate a program. But, if labels and a **Goto** were used instead, most would agree that this is a much more readable method.

```
procedure Error;
begin
  writeln;
  writeln('An error has occurred. You have asked this');
  writeln('program to print a file that does not exist.');
  writeln('Please locate the file and put the correct');
  writeln('drive and path as part of the command line.');
  Halt;
end;
```

EXIST

Exist is used in many of the programs in this book to check if a file exists in the designated path. The function returns a Boolean value and is so standardized that it can be used as an include library instead of hard coding it into all your applications.

If you prefer clarity, though, you may want to include the source text in each of your programs by using Turbo Pascal's editor. The editor has a block read command that can be used to fetch chunks of code that you use all the time.

```
function Exist (FileName : Name) : boolean;
var
  Fil       : text;

begin
  assign (Fil, FileName);
  {$I-} reset (Fil) {$I+};
  Exist := (IOresult = 0);
end;
```

FINDFIRST

The **FindFirst** procedure is necessary in any Turbo Pascal program that is used for reading a disk directory. It uses low-level machine hooks, through the Turbo **MsDos** interrupt call. All setup is performed through a register record.

The DOS function call that is used is number 78 (hex 4E). This call in conjunction with **FindNext** will give you the directory of a diskette.

```
procedure FindFirst;
begin
  Regs.AX := $4E00;
  Regs.DS := Seg(Mask);
  Regs.DX := Ofs(Mask) + 1;
  Regs.CX := Option;
  MSDos (Regs);
  ErrorCode := lo(Regs.AX);
end;
```

FINDNEXT

The **FindNext** procedure, like **FindFirst**, is necessary in any Turbo Pascal program that is used for reading a disk directory. Low-level coding is used. The Turbo **MsDos** call facilitates the procedure and, in fact, makes it possible in Pascal to include powerful routines like this one without an external declaration. All setup is performed through a register record.

The DOS function call that is used is number 79 (hex 4F). Calling this procedure repeatedly after a call to **FindFirst** will give you the directory of a diskette.

```
procedure FindNext;
begin
  Regs.AX := $4F00;
  Regs.CX := Option;
  MSDos (Regs);
  ErrorCode := lo(Regs.AX);
end;
```

HELP

Help is just a series of writes to the output device that tell the user of a utility how to use the utility. Since **Help** contains different text for each utility, it was not separated as an include library file (something that Turbo allows you to do and does very well). In general, though, this procedure is invoked when the user's command line input does not include any parameters.

Notice the use of **Halt** to terminate the program. Some Pascal purists would argue that it is a poor way to terminate a program. But, if labels and a **Goto** were used instead, most would agree that this is a much more readable method. The procedure **Error** uses the same technique.

```
procedure Help;
begin
  writeln;
  writeln('COLOR allows you to set the foreground,');
  writeln('background and border colors of you monitor.');
  writeln('To use it, just type COLOR followed by three');
```

(continued)

```pascal
    writeln('of the allowed parameters. ');
    writeln('Example: A>color red green brown');
    writeln;
    writeln('The following are valid parameters:');
    writeln;
    writeln('Black      Blue        Green      Cyan');
    writeln('Red        Magenta     Brown      LightGray');
    writeln('DarkGray   LightBlue   LightGreen LightCyan');
    writeln('LightRed   LightMagenta Yellow    White');
    Halt;
  end;
```

HEX

Hex takes a byte value and by picking up letters from an array can produce a string that is the hexadecimal representation of the byte. It is so straightforward that explaining it is almost ludicrous.

```pascal
function hex (decimalvalue : byte) : HexStr;
const
  map : array [0..15] of char = '0123456789ABCDEF';

var
  tmp : HexStr;

begin
  tmp[2] := map[(decimalvalue mod 16)];
  tmp[1] := map[(decimalvalue div 16)];
  tmp[0] := #2;                    {the length of the string}
  hex    := tmp;
end;
```

INITIALIZE

Initialize is a procedure that is found in many of the programs in this book. It is a particularly active procedure in Pmode, **Laser**, **Help**, and **Color** where large arrays must be initialized. The following example was taken from the program **Diag**.

```pascal
procedure Initialize;
begin
  AllChars   := [0..127];
  Exceptions := [0..8,11,12,14..31,43,46,127];
  Print      := AllChars - Exceptions;
end;
```

MACHINETYPE

All IBM machines and many of the compatibles have a machine type identification byte located in the ROM-BIOS chip. This byte can be found on such diverse machines as an Erikson PC and a Televideo AT. The **MachineType** procedure uses absolute memory references to mimic the BASIC function PEEK and obtain the value of the ID byte. It can accurately predict the type of machine that the program is running on.

```
procedure MachineType;
var
  MachineID : byte absolute $F000:$FFFE;

begin
  write('Machine ID         : ');
  case MachineID of
    255 : writeln('PC');
    254 : writeln('XT, Portable PC or Corona');
    253 : writeln('PCjr');
    252 : writeln('AT');
    251 : writeln('IBM XT / Enhanced Keyboard');
    249 : writeln('IBM Convertible');
    154 : writeln('Compaq Plus');
     45 : writeln('Compaq');
    else    writeln(MachineID);
  end;
end;
```

MOVEIT

The **MoveIt** procedure uses the standard Turbo Pascal procedure called **Rename** to move a file's directory entry from one path to another. Turbo must use a call to DOS function 56H (decimal 86), because this is the function that renames and moves files. Although DOS has this feature internally, none of the DOS commands use it.

```
procedure MoveIt;
var
  Fil    : file;

begin
  assign(Fil, FileInCurrentLocation);
  rename(Fil, FileInFutureLocation);
end;
```

OPENFILES

The **OpenFiles** procedure is pretty standard in all the utilities that open files for input or output. It uses the standard Turbo Pascal open file command.

```
procedure OpenFiles;
begin
  assign (WorkNameIn, FileIn);
  reset (WorkNameIn);
  assign (WorkNameOut, FileOut);
  rewrite (WorkNameOut);
end;
```

PARSECOMMANDLINE

The **ParseCommandLine** procedure checks for input on the DOS command line. Under various circumstances, this procedure has been modified in each utility to perform slightly differently. It uses some Turbo 3.0 features to return the number of parameters that were input at the command line and what they are.

In most of these utilities, if nothing is found on the command line, then the **Help** procedure is executed.

```
procedure ParseCommandLine;
begin
  if ParamCount = 0
    then Help
    else
      begin
        HelpCode := ParamStr (1);
        HelpCode := UpItsCase (HelpCode);
      end;
end;
```

PRINTLN

Println is used in place of the Turbo Pascal procedure **writeln** in the program **Funkeys**. Turbo apparently bypasses DOS for screen output and instead relies on the ROM-BIOS interrupt, which is fine for almost all programs but not for **Funkeys**. It requires that certain strings be passed to the DOS driver ANSI.SYS for proper interpretation as redefinition commands and strings.

What this all boils down to is that **Funkeys** needs this specialized screen output routine so that DOS understands the escape codes that the program outputs. DOS function 9 is used for the output. All strings that are output with this procedure must end with a $. The DOS function requires this character as an end-of-string marker.

```
procedure PrintIn(Instring : string255);
begin
  Regs.DX := Ofs(Instring)+1;
  Regs.DS := Seg(Instring);
  Regs.AH := 9;
  MsDos(Regs);
end;
```

ROMDATE

The **RomDate** procedure uses absolute memory accesses to scan an area of the ROM chip that usually holds the date that the ROM chip was developed. The date is usually stored in ASCII with a dash to separate the components. This routine has worked well with all machines tested. An Erikson PC, however, showed a strange sequence of characters where the date should be.

```
procedure RomDate;
type
  datemem  = array [0..7] of char;

var
  date    : datemem absolute $F000:$FFF5;
  i       : byte;
begin
  write('ROM BIOS Date        : ');
  for i := 0 to 7 do write(date[i]);
end;
```

SECTORWRITE

SectorWrite writes a sector into the buffer by using a ROM-BIOS interrupt. All preparations for the call to the BIOS are done by setting the appropriate registers. The only difference between this function and **SectorRead** is that the AH register is set to a 3 instead of a 2. Both of these routines are in the program **Disect**.

The two functions could be condensed into one and a parameter fed to it that tells it whether it is a read or write. For the purpose of clarity, they have been separated here.

```
function SectorWrite (

      var
        DriveNumber  : integer;
        TrackNumber  : integer;
        HeadNumber   : integer;
        SectorNumber : integer ) : byte;  {status code returned}

begin
  Regs.ES := Seg(SectorBuffer);
  Regs.BX := Ofs(SectorBuffer);
  Regs.CH := TrackNumber;
  Regs.CL := SectorNumber;
  Regs.DH := HeadNumber;
  Regs.DL := DriveNumber;
  Regs.AH := 3;  {write a sector}
  Regs.AL := 1;
  Intr (19,Regs);           {Rom-Bios service - Hex 13}
  SectorWrite := Regs.AH;
end;
```

SETDTA

SetDTA tells DOS what area of memory to use as a buffer for its transfer of data. The area called DTA is a record that is precisely broken up into meaningful entries.

This procedure is used in conjunction with the **FindFirst** and **FindNext** procedures to find all the directory entries on a given diskette or directory path.

```
procedure SetDTA;
begin
  Regs.AX := $1A00;
  Regs.DS := Seg(DTA);
  Regs.DX := Ofs(DTA);
  MSDos (Regs);
end;
```

UPITSCASE

UpItsCase is a function that takes a string of any length and sets all of the characters in the string to uppercase. It is a necessity when you are going to compare strings and case does not matter. Turbo's **Upcase** function is used to get the uppercase equivalent of each letter in a given string.

```
function UpItsCase (SourceStr : MaxString) : MaxString;
var
  I     : integer;

begin
  for I := 1 to length(SourceStr) do
    SourceStr[I] := UpCase(SourceStr[I]);
  UpItsCase := SourceStr
end;
```

YES

Yes returns a true or false depending on the input string **Answer**. This function is useful when evaluating user input.

```
function Yes : boolean;
var
  i : byte;

begin
  for i := 1 to length(Answer) do Answer[i] := UpCase (Answer[i]);
  if (Answer = 'Y') or (Answer = 'YES')
    then Yes := TRUE
    else Yes := FALSE;
end;
```

APPENDIX A

How to Compile

Compiling the source code provided with each utility in this book is a very easy procedure. If you use the following steps, you should not have any trouble converting the source files into executable machine code files.

Loading the Turbo Pascal Compiler

Type **turbo** at the DOS prompt. After a few seconds the following screen will show up:

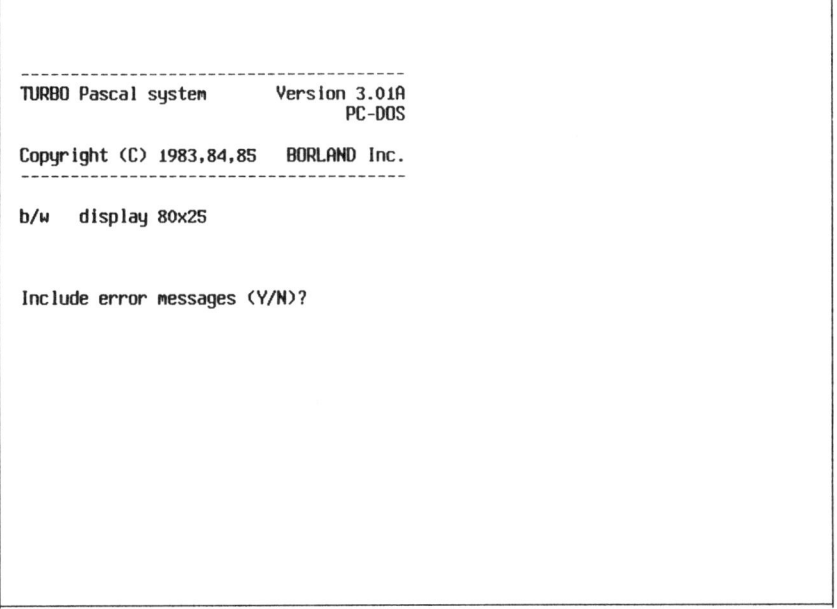

```
----------------------------------------
TURBO Pascal system      Version 3.01A
                                  PC-DOS

Copyright (C) 1983,84,85   BORLAND Inc.
----------------------------------------

b/w    display 80x25


Include error messages (Y/N)?
```

To make your life easier, type a **Y** to include the error messages. Don't be alarmed if your screen is slightly different from the one displayed, because you may have a different version of the Turbo compiler or may have it installed for a different type of display. After choosing **Y** or **N**, the following screen will be displayed:

```
Logged drive: A
Active directory: \

Work file:
Main file:

Edit      Compile  Run   Save

Dir       Quit compiler Options

Text:      0 bytes
Free: 62024 bytes

>
```

At this point you can remove the Turbo Pascal disk from drive A (if that is the drive that you are using it in) and begin typing one of the utilities into the Turbo Pascal editor. If you have purchased the source code diskette, place it in the drive. From the Turbo Pascal menu that is displayed on the screen, you will load one of the utilities from the disk. Just for practice, load the one called **LPRINT.PAS**. The way to do this is by pressing **W** on the main menu. Once you do so, the screen will display the following:

```
Logged drive: A
Active directory: \

Work file:
Main file:

Edit    Compile Run    Save

Dir     Quit  compiler Options

Text:     0 bytes
Free: 62024 bytes

>

Work file name:
```

Now type **lprint.pas**. The following will be displayed:

```
Logged drive: A
Active directory: \

Work file:
Main file:

Edit     Compile  Run   Save

Dir      Quit  compiler Options

Text:     0 bytes
Free: 62024 bytes

>

Work file name: lprint.pas

Loading A:\LPRINT.PAS
>
```

If you want to edit the file, you now simply type **E** (for edit) and you will be in the Turbo Pascal editor. Borland chose to make the Turbo editor work with the WordStar command set because so many people already know it. If you are not one of these many, then you should take some time to read over the beginning chapters of your Turbo Pascal Reference Manual. The reference manual lists each command and explains what it does in a clear and concise manner. Assuming that you do know how to navigate around a file with the Turbo editor, you are then ready to make changes in the source code and compile new command files. If you press **E** from the main menu in Turbo Pascal after loading the LPRINT.PAS source code file, you will see the following:

```
       Line 1    Col 1    Insert    Indent   A:LPRINT.PAS
Program Lprint;
{
        Title            : LINE PRINTING PROGRAM    Version 2.00
        Author           : Robert Alonso
        Versions         : 1.00 September 27, 1985
                           2.00 October 7, 1985

        Purpose          : This program prints out a line of text
                           to the line printer.

        I/O Requirements : The program requires text input from the
                           command line of an MS-DOS or PC-DOS
                           computer. The line of text is then sent
                           to the line printer. Ideally, the printer
                           should be connected and on before executing
                           this program.
}


var
  CommandString : string[127] absolute cseg : $80;

                { An absolute string is used to extract the input
                  from the DOS command line because the Turbo Pascal
```

Feel free to modify the source code as much as you want. You can personalize each utility to print out your name on the screen or to work with different hardware or in conjunction with other software products. The only limit is your imagination. If you are interested in learning about Turbo Pascal and how to design useful utilities, then you can use the utilities in this book as examples. Just study the source code carefully.

Eventually, you will want to compile these modifications into working command files. This is easily accomplished by returning to the Turbo Pascal main menu. To get there, just press the **Control** key followed by **KD**. This procedure will take you out of edit mode and into the main menu. You will see the following displayed:

```
Logged drive: A
Active directory: \

Work file: A:\LPRINT.PAS
Main file:

Edit      Compile Run   Save

Dir       Quit  compiler Options

Text: 3126 bytes
Free: 58898 bytes

>
```

To proceed from here, you will have to go to the compiler options submenu. In the submenu you can choose to compile your source code in memory or out to disk in a command file format. These choices are important because compiling from the main menu will default to memory mode, which means that you can run only the compiled code from memory and that when you exit the Turbo Pascal compiler all your compiled code will be lost. The submenu will display the following:

```
compile -> Memory
           Com-file
           cHn-file

command line Parameters:

Find run-time error   Quit
>
```

To compile to the disk, type **C** for Com-file. Once you type "C" the screen will change quickly and display the following, which you can disregard:

```
                Memory
compile -> Com-file
           cHn-file


minimum cOde segment size:    0000 (max 0D28 paragraphs)
minimum Data segment size:    0000 (max 0FDC paragraphs)
mInimum free dynamic memory: 0400 paragraphs
mAximum free dynamic memory: A000 paragraphs


Find run-time error   Quit

>
```

The next step is to type "Q" to quit from the submenu and go to the main menu. Everything is now set for you to compile the source code into a command file. Just type **C** from the main menu, and Turbo Pascal will begin compiling your source code into machine code. If any errors are encountered in your source code, Turbo will stop compiling and give you a warning message. It will then display the approximate location where the error occurred. If nothing goes wrong, the following screen will be displayed while compiling:

```
Logged drive: A
Active directory: \

Work file: A:\LPRINT.PAS
Main file:

Edit     Compile  Run   Save

Dir      Quit  compiler Options

Text:  3126 bytes
Free: 58898 bytes

>

Compiling --> A:\LPRINT.COM
   103 lines

Code:       0020 paragraphs (   512 bytes), 0D08 paragraphs free
Data:       0002 paragraphs (    32 bytes), 0FDA paragraphs free
Stack/Heap: 0400 paragraphs ( 16384 bytes) (minimum)
            A000 paragraphs (655360 bytes) (maximum)

>
```

If you've done everything in steps up to now, you will have a file called LPRINT.COM stored on the disk in drive A. The same steps that were used to create this command file can be used to create all the other utilities in this book.

APPENDIX B

Installing the Compiled Utilities

If you purchased the compiled utilities on disk, you should place them on your hard disk by following the instructions provided here.

Making a Backup to a Hard Disk

1. At the **C>** prompt, type **cd **.
2. Next type **md \tutil**.
3. Type **cd \tutil**.
4. Insert the Turbo Pascal Utilities Disk in A.
5. Type **copy a: *.***.
6. When the prompt returns, you will have a backup in a subdirectory called tutil.

Now that you have the utilities stored on your hard disk, you can tell the disk operating system to look in the subdirectory where you placed them every time you type in a command. DOS, the disk operating system, has a command that enables you to specify where it will search for external commands that you want executed. If you tell DOS exactly where the utilities are, you can use them while you are in any subdirectory or the root directory (the main directory) or even while you are using another drive altogether. This feature can save you time as well as make the utilities more handy.

The command's name is *path*. It is an internal command that is built into the DOS command processor and therefore is always accessible to DOS. The path command can be placed in your autoexec.bat file. If you include the path command in the autoexec.bat file, then every time you boot your computer from the hard disk, the path command will be automatically executed and the operating system will know where to look for the Turbo Pascal utilities. In the following section is an example of how to set up the path command.

Setting Up a Path Command

1. At the **C>** prompt type **cd **.

2. Next type **dir autoexec.bat**.

3. If the computer prints out the following, then you don't have an autoexec.bat file and need to create one. Step 5 shows you how to do this. Skip step 4.

   Volume in drive C is ????????
   Directory of C: \

   File not found

4. If the preceding was not printed on the screen, you must edit your autoexec.bat file to include the path command that is shown in step 6. Use a word processor to do the editing. Skip the rest of the steps.

5. At the **C>** prompt, type **copy con:autoexec.bat** and press return.

6. The cursor should now be blinking under the letter C. Everything that you type from this point on will be copied from the keyboard into a file called autoexec.bat. Type **path c: \ ;c: \ tutil** to make DOS always look in the root directory of the hard drive as well as in the subdirectory we created to store the utilities; called tutil.

7. Now type **CTRL-Z** and press the return key. The file will be saved, and the next time that your computer is turned on, the path command will be automatically executed and you will be able to use the utilities from any subdirectory you choose.

Index

A

ALTER, 77, 79
ANSI.SYS, 19, 20, 142
Applications
   COPYIIPC, 94
   Lotus 1-2-3, 24, 36, 37, 61, 62, 67
   Sidekick, 9, 55
   Volkswriter, 36
   WordStar, 36, 37, 72, 73
ASCII, 44, 50, 56, 72, 73, 128, 129
ATTRIB.EXE, 77

B

Backup, 157
BASIC, 1, 2, 67, 141
Batch file, 4, 5, 37
BEEP, 4, 5
BIOS, 19, 20, 84–86, 130, 132, 141–143
Blaise Pascal, 1

C

CAL, 9, 10
CAPS LOCK, 36, 37
CHMOD, 78
COLOR, 13, 14, 140
Color monitor, 13
COMMAND.COM, 3
Compaq, 84, 88
Compile, 147–155
CONFIG.SYS, 19, 20
COPYIIPC, 94
Corona PC, 37, 88
COUNT, 44, 45
CREATE, 50, 51

D

DETAB, 55, 56
DIAG, 84, 85
DISECT, 94, 95, 143
Disk Transfer Area (DAT), 103

E

EDLIN, 50
ENCODE, 60, 62, 136
Epson printers, 122
Erikson PC, 141, 143

F

FAT, 95
File Utilities
   COUNT, 44, 45
   CREATE, 50, 51
   DETAB, 55, 56
   ENCODE, 60, 62, 136
   LLIST, 67, 68
   WSASCII, 72, 73
FINDFILE, 103, 104

Functions
  ConvertToScalar, 16, 131
  Exist, 42, 52, 56, 62, 69, 73, 114, 138
  Hex, 97, 140
  SectorRead, 96, 143
    SectorWrite, 96, 143, 144
    UpItsCase, 16, 25, 38, 79, 105, 118, 124, 145
  Yes, 97, 145
FUNKEYS, 19, 21, 142, 143

G

General Utilities
  BEEP, 4, 5
  CAL, 9, 10
  COLOR, 13, 14, 140
  LPRINT, 41, 149, 150–152, 155
  FUNKEYS, 19, 21, 142, 143
  HELP, 24, 140
  KEYS, 36, 37
Genicom 3014, 122

H

Hard disk, 103, 157
Hardware
  Color monitor, 13
  Compaq, 84, 88
  Corona PC, 37, 88
  Epson printers, 122
  Erikson PC, 141, 143
  Genicom 3014, 122
  Hard disk, 103, 157
  Hewlett Packard LaserJet, 2, 116, 117
  IBM
    AT, 84, 88
    Convertible, 84, 88
    Display, 13, 122
    Enhanced Keyboard, 88
    Graphics Printer, 2, 122
    PC, 1, 84, 88, 93
    PCjr, 2, 84, 88
    Portable PC, 88
    Proprinter, 122
    XT, 84, 88
  Monochrome monitor, 13
  NEC
    P5, 122
    P7, 122
    V–20, 84
  Okidata printers, 122
  Televideo AT, 141
  Texas Instruments
    99/4 Impact printer, 122
  Wang PM-0016, 122
HELP, 24, 140
Hewlett Packard LaserJet, 2, 116, 117

I

IBM
  AT, 84, 88
  Convertible, 84, 88
  Display, 13, 122
  Enhanced Keyboard, 88
  Graphics Printer, 2, 122
  PC, 1, 84, 88, 93
  PCjr, 2, 84, 88
  Portable PC, 88
  Proprinter, 122
  XT, 84, 88
IBMBIO.COM, 19
IBMDOS.COM, 19
Installation, 157–158
Intel, 135

K

KEYS, 36, 37

L

LASER, 116, 117, 140
LIM, 135
LLIST, 67, 68
Lotus 1-2-3, 24, 36, 37, 61, 62, 67
LPRINT, 41, 149, 150-152, 155
LPT1, 41

M

Microsoft, 2, 4, 77, 91, 103, 122, 129, 135
Monochrome monitor, 13
MOVE, 112, 113
MS-DOS, 2-4, 6, 14, 21, 24-25, 42, 45, 52, 56, 62, 68, 73, 77, 79, 85, 104, 113, 117, 123, 129
MSDOS.SYS, 19

N

NEC
  P5, 122
  P7, 122
  V-20, 84
Niklaus Wirth, 1
NUM LOCK, 36, 37

O

Okidata printers, 122

P

.PRN, 67
Pascal, Blaise, 1
Path command, 158
PC-DOS, 3, 6, 14, 19, 21, 24, 25, 42, 45, 52, 56, 62, 68, 73, 79, 85, 104, 113, 117, 123, 129
Peripheral Utilities
  LASER, 116, 117, 140
  PMODE, 116, 122, 123, 140

PMODE, 116, 122, 123, 140
POST, 19
Procedures
  AskForEdit, 100
  AskForInput, 99
  BeepTone, 7, 128, 129
  CallChmod, 82, 129
  ChangeColors, 18
  CheckEquipmentList, 92
  CheckMemorySize, 91, 130
  ClearFrame, 99
  CloseFiles, 48, 59, 66, 70, 76, 131
  Convert_All_Input_To_Scalars, 18
  ConvertCharacters, 76
  ConvertToScalar, 28, 40, 81, 120, 126
  Copyright, 86, 132
  CountCharacters, 48
  CountLines, 48
  CountWords, 48
  CreateFile, 54
  DiskDrives, 88
  Display, 99
  DisplayEdit, 101
  DisplayEntry, 108
  DisplayRuler, 54
  DoDirSubs, 110
  DoIO, 71, 134
  DoSubs, 109
  DOSversion, 90, 134, 135
  EmsCheck, 91, 135
  EncodeCharacters, 66, 136
  EncodePassword, 165
  Error, 6, 11, 15, 26, 38, 63, 68, 74, 80, 97, 114, 118, 124, 128, 137, 139
  ExtractAttributeValue, 82
  FindFirst, 107, 138, 144
  FindNext, 108, 139, 144
  FrameIt, 98
  GameAdapter, 89
  GetCommandLine, 42

GetDirectories, 110
GetEntries, 109
GetWriteCharacters, 54
Help, 6, 11, 15, 22, 38, 42, 46, 52, 57,
    64, 69, 74, 80, 106, 114, 119, 125, 128,
    139, 142
Initialize, 17, 23, 27, 38, 47, 75, 81,
    85, 98, 106, 119, 125, 140
MachineType, 87, 141
MoveIt, 115, 141
NoFiles, 106
OpenFile, 47, 58, 65, 70, 75, 142
OutputResults, 49
_PROCS, 28–34
ParseCommandLine, 17, 27, 38, 46,
    53, 57, 64, 70, 74, 81, 106, 115, 120,
    126, 128, 142
ParseDTA, 108
ParseLine, 7, 11
PerformanceIndex, 90
PrintCommandLine, 43
PrintControlCodes, 121, 126
PrintCrLf, 43
Printers, 88
PrintEscapeSequences, 23
PrintHeading, 93
PrintHelpText, 34
Println, 22, 142, 143
ProcessData, 12
ProduceSound, 7
ProgHelp, 26
ReadDiskAndMakeEdits, 101
ReportResult, 12
RomDate, 86, 143
ScanAndOutput, 59
ScanForDirectories, 109
SearchForFile, 47, 53, 58, 65, 75
SerialPorts, 89
SetDTA, 107, 144

SetTheMode, 40
SubMessage, 80
VideoMode, 89
WriteBuffer, 102
Programs
  ALTER, 77, 79
  BEEP, 4, 5
  CAL, 9, 10
  COLOR, 13, 14, 140
  COUNT, 44, 45
  CREATE, 50, 51
  DETAB, 55, 56
  DIAG, 84, 85
  DISECT, 94, 95, 143
  ENCODE, 60, 62, 136
  FINDFILE, 103, 104
  FUNKEYS, 19, 21, 142, 143
  HELP, 24, 140
  KEYS, 36, 37
  LASER, 116, 117, 140
  LLIST, 67, 68
  LPRINT, 41, 149, 150–152, 155
  MOVE, 112, 113
  PMODE, 116, 122, 123, 140
  WSASCII, 72, 73

R

ROM, 19, 20, 84–86, 130, 132, 141–143

S

Sidekick, 9, 55
System Utilities
  ALTER, 77, 79
  DIAG, 84, 85
  DISECT, 94, 95, 143
  FINDFILE, 103, 104
  MOVE, 112, 113

T

Televideo AT, 141
Texas Instruments, 99/4 Impact printer, 122

V

Volkswriter, 36

W

Wang PM-0016, 122
Wirth, Niklaus, 1
WordStar, 36, 37, 72, 73
WSASCII, 72, 73

Tired of Typing?

Order the Turbo Pascal utilities in this book on disk and you won't have to worry about typing them in or about making any mistakes while typing them in. For $19.95, you will get two diskettes, one with the source code as it appears in this book and the other with the compiled utilities.

If you don't own the Turbo Pascal compiler, these two disks can save you the expense of having to buy it. Since the utilities are provided in compiled form, you don't need to purchase the compiler unless you plan on modifying the utilities.

A check or money order is preferred, but you can also use your Visa or MasterCard. If you are using a credit card, include your card number, expiration date and signature. For personal checks, allow two weeks for processing.

Send order to:

> Robert Alonso
> Turbo Pascal Disks
> 17 Church Street, Suite 10
> Nutley, NJ 07110

Please send me _____copies of TURBO PASCAL UTILITIES.

☐ Check or money order enclosed for $19.95 (Shipping & handling included)

Charge my credit card...   ☐ MasterCard   ☐ Visa

Card Number _____Expiration Date _____

Signature (Order invalid unless signed) _____

Name (please print) _____

Title _____Company _____

Address _____

City _____State _____Zip Code _____

Phone Number (daytime) _____

Prices and Terms Subject to Change Without Notice